I'm Fired?!?

I'm Fired?!?

A Business Fable about the Challenges of Losing One Job and Finding Another

by Roger Dusing

Lighthouse Point Press
Pittsburgh, Pennsylvania

I'm Fired?!?:
A Business Fable about the Challenges of Losing
One Job and Finding Another
Roger Dusing

© 2015 Roger Dusing

ALL RIGHTS RESERVED

Except as permitted under U.S. Copyright Act of 1976, no part of this publication may be reproduced, distributed or transmitted in any form or by any means, or stored in a database or retrieval system without the prior written consent of the author.

Published by Lighthouse Point Press
Pittsburgh, Pennsylvania

www.lighthousepointpress.com

www.im-fired.com

ISBN: 978-0-9792998-2-7

Printed in the United States of America

Dedicated to my loving wife, who has supported me more than I deserve during my too many times in the job search process.

CONTENTS

Foreword	ix
Chapter 1 - The News	1
Chapter 2 - Fear	9
Chapter 3 - The Family	15
Chapter 4 - Outplacement	19
Chapter 5 - Networking 101	31
Chapter 6 – Putting It In Writing	43
Chapter 7 – Blowing Your Own Horn	55
Chapter 8 - Telling the Tale	63
Chapter 9 - The Interview	73
Chapter 10 - On My Own	81
Chapter 11 - Which Way to Go?	89
Chapter 12 - Lessons Learned	103
My Reflections	107

Appendices

    A – 30 Interview Questions You Need to be Ready to Answer   117

    B – Sample Accomplishments for Your Resume   121

    C – Bob's First Resume   126

    D – Bob's Revised Resume   127

About the Author   128

Praise for I'm Fired?!?   129

FOREWORD

Anyone who has ever lost a job and survived the emotional ups and downs of seeking a new one will immediately identify with Bob Smith, the ultimate hero of Roger Dusing's timely and informative book. Bob's story is one that millions of Americans have experienced – being blindsided by a downsizing, suffering the loss of a major piece of one's identity, dealing with financial worries, trying to focus clearly on what to do next, struggling with practical aspects of resume writing, fielding tough interview questions, negotiating salary, and how to make the best use of this thing called "outplacement."

Roger Dusing knows whereof he speaks – he has survived the loss of six jobs and has recovered – and learned – from every one. *I'm Fired?!?* traces the steps of Roger's composite alter-ego as he struggles and is enlightened along the way. He quickly realizes that there is a better way to seek re-employment than he (and most people) ever know. After all, most of us never took a college course on Career Transition or Job-Hunting 101.

Bob discovers that he suffers from common myths and misconceptions about the job market, networking, and how to write a resume. *I'm Fired?!?* offers the best of two things we like most about good business books – a compelling story we can follow and relate to, and practical insights and tips we can use, including appendices containing, among other valuable notes, a list of interview questions and Bob's before-and-after resumes.

Having spent much of my own career as a job-search and career-transition consultant with two major outplacement firms, I can attest that readers of *I'm Fired?!?* will be well advised. I welcome this heartfelt and enlightening contribution to our collective library of job search literature.

Leigh Branham
Founder/Principal, Keeping the People, Inc.

CHAPTER 1 – THE NEWS

Bob knew something was going on. Alice, the department Vice President, had been acting strange these last few days. She seemed distracted and was almost always in meetings with the executive team. This morning she had been flitting around the office talking to almost everyone, except Bob.

At the coffee pot, Bob heard that several big meetings had been scheduled for later that day. Most employees had been told to meet in the conference room at either 2 or 3 o'clock. Bob, and several of his peers, hadn't heard anything. He was starting to get a little nervous himself.

As usual, Bob ate his lunch at his desk while he looked over the *Wall Street Journal*. He tried to keep up with the financial news as best he could. Just as he was throwing away his sandwich wrappers, Alice stopped by his office.

"Bob," she said a little nervously, "can I see you in my office for a minute, please?"

"Sure, just let me clean up. Do I need to bring anything?"

"Uh, no," she replied. "I don't think so."

A few minutes later, Bob and Alice were seated at the small conference table in her office. Bob could see signs of stress in her eyes. Whatever they were going to talk about didn't seem easy for her to say.

"Bob, as you know, sales have been off for the first two quarters this year. In addition, our planned acquisition of G-Tech seems to have failed. It looks like they got a better offer that we can't afford to match. What that means is that we have more staff now than we need and I'm afraid we are going to have to eliminate some jobs."

Bob considered what Alice had said and his self-preservation instincts kicked in. "I was afraid that might happen, so I have been looking over my staff and I think I may have some suggestions…"

Alice cut him off. "Bob, thank you, but we've already reviewed the staff and determined how we want to restructure. We have meetings scheduled with the entire company this afternoon to announce the new organization."

"Which meeting do you want me to attend?" Bob asked hopefully.

Alice collected herself before she started. "Bob, part of the reorganization involves a reduction in force. We have decided to flatten our organization structure and your position has been eliminated."

Bob felt like he had just been punched in the stomach. His head swam. Bob had been with National Products for 15 years. He knew the acquisition of G-Tech was not going well and he knew that the company might have to lay off some people. But he never thought it might be him.

"Bob, I know this is a surprise for you, and it's news that nobody wants to hear. We have prepared a package of severance and benefits continuation to help carry you – hopefully until you can find another job."

I'm Fired?!?

Bob started to regain his focus and the news began to sink in. "I'm fired?!? Why me?" he asked. "I've been here for 15 years, all my performance appraisals have been 'meets' or 'exceeds expectations,' and I've got almost perfect attendance. Why me? You need me." The anxiety in his voice was obvious.

Alice thought back to the training she'd had for this meeting and looked at the outline she had prepared. Knowing that people would react to this news, the company hired an outplacement counselor to assist employees who lost their jobs. That counselor also had provided some training to Alice and the other executives who had to deliver the bad news. She tried to be as calm as possible. "Bob, you have been an excellent employee for 15 years, and we truly appreciate everything you've done for the company. Please understand, including you in this reduction-in-force is not a reflection on your contributions or your performance, but on our staffing needs. We just don't need as many supervisors as we did before."

Bob was getting angry. "Well, who else did you fire? What about Simmons? He hasn't carried his own weight for years!"

"Try to calm down, Bob. I want to keep this conversation focused on you." Alice stayed as professional as she could, but Bob could tell that she agreed with him about Simmons. "You and I have never talked about the performance of the other supervisors, and we don't need to start now. Let me just say that you are not the only one affected.

"We have eliminated about 20 jobs from various parts of the company, including several others in Finance. Let's just talk about you and how we can help you move on to another opportunity."

"Well, why do I have to go? You're going to need Financial Analysts and Accountants, aren't you? What if I go back to my old job? Shirley is going to have a baby in four months. You'll need someone like me to fill in for her. Why don't you just terminate her now? Her performance isn't that great and she'd probably like the time to spend with the baby. That's a plan. You fire Shirley, and I'll take her job."

"We have considered lots of options and are confident that the best choice for National Products, and for you, is for us to help you find a new opportunity with another company." Even as Alice said it, the words sounded a little hollow to her, but that is what the counselor said she needed to say. But now Alice talked from her heart. "Look, Bob, you know you wouldn't be happy going backwards in your career. You have grown into a very good supervisor, and while the job market may be tight, you know what you're good at. Nobody likes change, and it's tough to leave a place where you've been for so long – but it's really the best way. You can take your skills and market them anywhere. You'll be okay. This happened to me once and in the end, I had a better job and made more money. Calm down and let's talk about how we can help you move on."

The anger was fading, and Bob was beginning to accept the news. He didn't like it, but he was starting to understand there wasn't much he could do about it. "Okay," he said with a bitter sigh. "What will National Products do to help me 'find a new career'?"

Alice breathed a little easier. Even though there was some sarcasm in Bob's last statement, she could finally move the conversation forward. "To start with, National Products has put together a salary continuation package. Today is Wednesday, the 14th. We'll consider your official termination date as Friday, the 30th. That's just over two weeks. We would have asked you for two weeks' notice if you had resigned, so we'll pay you two weeks of in-lieu-of-notice. After that, we'll give you 15 weeks of severance pay. That is one week for every complete year of service you have given us. We think that is fair and hopefully will provide you with enough time to find another job. Of course, we'll also pay you for the two weeks of vacation you haven't used yet.

"Will all that be in a lump sum?" Bob was thinking about getting a check for almost four months of pay. What would the taxes be on that? How would he budget that kind of cash flow?

"No, it won't be a lump sum. We'll continue to pay you through our regular payroll cycles and we'll continue your direct deposit. On the 30th you'll get two checks, one for your pay-in-lieu-of-notice and one for your vacation. Then on the 15th and last day of each month you'll get your severance checks until the 15 weeks have been exhausted."

"What if I find another job before then, will I still get all of the severance?" Bob asked hopefully.

"Yes," Alice responded. "We'll pay out all of the severance, even if you are working somewhere else before it expires."

"What about my benefits?" Bob asked. His wife, Linda, had a doctor's appointment for later that week. She was concerned about a mole on her shoulder. "Will I still have medical insurance?"

"We will continue both your medical insurance and dental through the severance period. During that time we will continue to pay our share of the premiums and will deduct your share from your severance checks. After your severance period has expired, you will be able to continue your insurance through COBRA. Human Resources will be in touch with you before then to explain all of that. As I understand it, you will have to pay the full premium, but the insurance can continue for another year or so, I think." Alice was getting outside of her expertise and didn't want to commit to anything she wasn't sure of.

"Anything else?" Bob asked.

"Yes," said Alice gratefully. "One of the best benefits yet. National Products has agreed to supply you with a full outplacement program."

Bob was skeptical. "What does "full outplacement" mean? Does it mean they will find me a job?"

Alice pulled out a brochure that she had been given by the counselor. "They won't find you a job, but they will teach you how to find one. This brochure explains it better than I can, but basically you will be provided with an office, administrative support, and telephone and computer access. More importantly, they also will provide coaching and counseling, conduct some career assessments, and train you how to look for a job."

Bob slid the brochure across the desk and glanced though it. The whole discussion was starting to overwhelm him. "When do you want me to clean out my desk? Do I get to say good-bye to anyone?" Depression was beginning to sink in.

Alice seemed relieved that the conversation was winding down. "Here's a letter that Human Resources put together that explains everything I told you – the severance, vacation pay, benefits, etc. Why don't you take the letter, and this brochure, and go home now. Talk with Linda and try to get comfortable with the situation. I've arranged an appointment for you at 10 o'clock tomorrow morning with the outplacement counselor. His name and his company's address and phone number are on the back of the brochure. After that meeting, call me and we'll find a time for you to get your things. If you'd like to do it during the day, that would be fine. If you'd rather return in the evening or over a weekend we can arrange that also.

"One last thing," Alice continued, "is that I ask that you not talk with any employees about this for the rest of today. We have other employees that we need to have this conversation with, and then we have our group meetings later today. We want to make sure that everyone hears about this from the company. I'm sure you can understand that."

"I understand, Alice," Bob answered. "Well, thank you for everything. I've enjoyed working for you and being a part of your team. I wish it hadn't turned out this way, but, oh well. I guess I'll call you tomorrow."

Alice was back to her old, friendly self. "Thank you, Bob. I really appreciate your efforts and I've enjoyed working with you. We'll miss you."

Bob collected his papers. He shook hands with Alice and walked slowly back to his cubicle. Everything seemed surreal – like he wasn't really there. It was all too strange. He'd worked for National Products for 15 years and now he was out on the street.

Bob turned off his computer, put his newspaper in his briefcase, picked up his lunchbox, and headed for the elevators. On the way out, he mumbled something to the receptionist about being out for the rest of the day, but she wasn't completely sure what he said. Bob walked slowly to his car and started thinking about the rest of his life.

CHAPTER 2 – FEAR

Bob climbed into his car. It was hot that day and the inside of the car was boiling. He rolled down the window, turned the air-conditioning on full blast and just sat there, wondering. What was he going to do?

As the car cooled down, Bob left the parking lot and pulled into the light, early-afternoon traffic. How was he going to tell Linda? She was a worrier, especially about money. He often joked that even if she won the Lottery she'd worry about making the next house payment. He had to approach her just right, and without the kids around. Timing would be everything.

His mom and dad would be a problem too. They were both approaching retirement and were very proud of his career with National Products. They were adjusting to living on a fixed income and starting to draw down their savings. Lately, he had started worrying about them and their finances. He certainly didn't want them to worry about him. Maybe he just wouldn't tell them anything now and wait until he found a new job.

Bob started day-dreaming. Where could he find a job? Where *should* he find a job? Was it time to get out of accounting? Maybe he could go work for CBF Industries, National's biggest competitor. That would show the folks at National! Of course

CBF didn't have much of an office locally, and he had always heard bad things about the work environment, but he needed to check it out. Maybe it was time to get out of manufacturing. The newspapers kept talking about the growth of service industries.

Maybe he should look in to one of those. But he didn't know anything about hotels or retail or health care. Why would they hire him? His day-dreams turned into nightmares and he started to imagine his family hungry, and homeless, and looking at him and shouting "It's all your fault!"

Cars were honking behind him and Bob realized he was sitting at a stop-light that was just turning yellow. He must have sat there through the green light. Oh, well. Where did he have to go? Maybe it was time to open his own bookkeeping business. He and Linda had talked about it years ago, when the children were young. He could keep the books for three or four small companies in his neighborhood. He would work out of his home office and be able to spend more time with the kids. It would be great. But, he wasn't a CPA, so that might keep some clients away. He wasn't much of a salesman, so getting new customers might be tough. He also wasn't sure if Linda would be okay with the uncertainty and the income fluctuation. Maybe he'd think about his own business later.

They would need to control expenses. First, they'd need to stop eating out as much. The kids would complain, and he thought jokingly that the price of McDonald's stock might fall, but that would be okay. Maybe he should cancel their membership to the swim club. The kids really enjoyed the pool and were on the swim team, but it was a luxury. Should they cancel cable TV? What about all those magazines Linda subscribed to? How much money did they really need to live on? If he had to take a salary cut, what could they afford? Bob drove past his exit letting all these scary questions run through his mind.

The questions continued to come, but the answers didn't. Bob pulled off the highway in a small town about 15 miles later. Despite his vow to stop spending money, he drove through a fast-food restaurant and bought some french-fries and a soft-drink. Sitting in the parking lot he noticed a bookstore in the neighboring strip mall. With time on his hands, he drove over, parked under a shade tree and went inside.

A bell over the door jingled as he went inside the small, cool store. A friendly looking elderly man looked up from behind the counter. "Can I help you find something?" he asked.

"No thanks, I'm just wandering." Bob mumbled. But then he paused and said, "Well, do you have anything about finding a job?"

"Sure," said the storekeeper, "There are several things in that back aisle. See that sign that says 'careers'? It's all there."

"Oh, I see it. Thanks." said Bob, and he walked to the back of the store. For such a small store, Bob was amazed at the amount of career material the store had. There were books on resumes, cover letters, interviewing, finding a job on the Internet, starting your own business, and more.

Bob selected a medium-priced book on resumes and cover letters, and walked back up to the counter. On a display stand, he saw a stack of the *Job News*, a local help-wanted publication, and he picked up a copy of that also. "Might as well get after it," he thought to himself.

"That's quite a collection of career material you have back there," Bob said as he laid his items on the counter. "I'm surprised to see that much stuff."

The storekeeper laughed. "I hear that a lot, but I only carry a few of the books that are published. The publishers are cranking out new books every day. It's amazing. Most of them also link to dedicated websites and blogs. Helping people find a job must be a big, and profitable, business. Did you find everything you wanted?"

"Yeah, thanks," answered Bob, handing him his credit card. He thought to himself that he needed to start using that card more carefully. Now was not a good time to be running up more debt. Especially at the interest rates the credit card companies charged.

"You looking for a new job?" the storekeeper asked.

Bob sighed. "As a matter-of-fact, I am. I just found out a few hours ago." He was surprised to find that it felt good to say it out loud.

"I'm sorry to hear that," the old man said shaking his head. "It seems like everyone is moving around so much these days. Well, good luck to you. I'm sure it will work out for you. Here's a free bookmark for you to use. It has the number of a local job-hunters' club on it. They give them to me to pass on to folks just like you. I hear they do a pretty good business."

Bob thanked the man, collected his purchases and walked back to his car. As he walked, he read the bookmark. **Lakeview Job-Hunters Club. A free support group for people looking to**

change careers or help others that are already in the process. Meetings Wednesdays at 9:30 AM at the Lakeview Christian Church. Join us! "Huh." Bob said aloud. "Who'd have thought?" Sipping his slightly watery drink, Bob headed for home.

CHAPTER 3 – THE FAMILY

"You got FIRED!?!" Linda was almost shouting. "How could you let this happen? What did you do? What are we going to do now?" She sat down heavily in the chair in their bedroom, glaring at Bob. It was about 5 o'clock that afternoon. Linda had been surprised to see Bob home that early. He asked her to join him in the bedroom while he changed clothes.

Bob slowly counted to five. "Linda, I didn't get fired. Like I said, my job got eliminated. I didn't do anything wrong. It's not my fault!" Now he was getting a little angry, too.

There was a knock at the door. "Is everything okay in there? I thought someone said FIRE. Is there a fire?" The nervous voice behind the door was Amy, Bob and Linda's 13-year-old daughter.

Bob smiled. "There's no fire, Honey. Your mom just said she was TIRED, very tired. Go back and watch TV."

"Okay… if you're sure." Amy replied.

"We're sure," said Linda. "I'm sorry, Bob. I am just so surprised. I mean, you've been there for 15 years. What's going on? Are they going out of business or something?" Linda was still stressed, but Amy's interruption had broken the ice.

Bob tried to explain. "Remember me talking about National planning to acquire G-Tech? Well, it didn't go through. We had hired additional staff to get ready for the acquisition, and now without G-Tech, we're over staffed. I think lots of people got RIFed."

"What does RIFed mean?" Linda asked.

"RIF stands for reduction-in-force. That means that jobs were eliminated and they don't plan on calling those people back if business picks up. It's kind of like a permanent layoff. People who were RIFed had their job eliminated."

"Why you though? You've been a good employee, haven't you? You've been getting increases and bonuses every year. Why didn't they cut out the new people? And what about that Simmons guy you're always complaining about. Is he still there?" Now Linda was getting angry again, but at least she seemed more upset with National Products than with Bob.

"I don't know who else was affected. Alice wouldn't tell me," Bob answered. "I kind of hope they cut Simmons, but he's been having some real problems at home with one of his kids. He really doesn't need to be looking for a job now."

"Like you do!" Linda interjected.

"I got cut because they eliminated my level. That must mean they cut all the Supervisors, or at least most of them. They were holding group meetings this afternoon. I'll probably be able to get the scoop out of Susan tomorrow." Susan Johnston was Bob's lead accountant. He hoped that she would still be there. Maybe she'd even get a small increase out of this if she had to pick up some of his duties.

"But, Bob, what are we going to do for money? What about insurance? I've just made the appointment to have this mole looked at. Why did this have to happen?" Linda sat back and began to cry. She was simply overwhelmed. "What if you can't find a job here? I don't want to lose the house. What are we going to tell the kids? What about our friends?" The tears increased.

Bob walked over, sat on the arm of the chair, and put his arms around her. "It'll be okay, Honey. They've given me a pretty good severance package. I'll be paid for about four months. They'll continue my insurance for all that time, then I can go on COBRA after that. They've also set me up with some consultant who is supposed to find me a job. I go there tomorrow morning and meet with them." Bob paused and let the enormity of what he just said wash over both of them. "We'll be okay. I have good skills. I picked up a book on job-hunting today. I'll get another job. We won't lose the house. Try not to worry. We'll get through this." They both sat there quietly for a while and stared out the window. They both hoped that he was right.

Dinner that night was homemade pizza.

"Kids," Bob started tentatively, "I wanted you to know that it looks like I'll be changing jobs here pretty soon."

"Oh, did you get a promotion or something?" asked Amy.

"No, I'll be leaving National Products. They announced a reorganization today and my job was eliminated. I'll be looking for a job with another company," Bob replied.

Andy perked up. "Which other company?"

Bob smiled. "I don't know yet, son. I've got to find a new job."

"Won't that take a long time?" asked Amy. "Will we run out of money?" Her eyes were getting wider and a note of panic was creeping into her voice. "What am I going to tell my friends? When I go back to school this fall and a teacher asks 'Amy, what does your father do?', I am NOT going to just smile and say, 'He's unemployed.' I just WON'T DO IT!"

Bob was reassuring. "Calm down, Honey. There's lots of time before you go back to school. National Products is going to keep paying me for some time while I look for a job. We won't run out of money and I'm sure I'll have a new job before your friends even find out. After all, how many of them know, or even care, what I do or who I work for? We'll be just fine."

A worried look crossed Andy's face. "Will you still be able to coach Little League?"

Bob laughed. Sometimes it was good to get things back into perspective.

CHAPTER 4 – OUTPLACEMENT

The next morning Bob's alarm went off at the usual time. As he started to get out of bed he remembered that he wasn't going to work today. His appointment with the outplacement counselor wasn't until 10 o'clock. He could sleep in. This was going to take some getting used to.

After a shower and a leisurely breakfast, Bob was in his car driving back downtown. The outplacement company was in a business park, just about 15 minutes from National Products. He almost wished it was farther away.

After dinner the night before, he had spent some time in his den getting organized. He hadn't updated his resume in years, so he worked on a new one. He tried to model it after one he'd seen in the book he'd bought that afternoon. He wasn't satisfied, but it was a start.

At 9:50 he parked his car in front of Genesis Career Counseling and went inside. The lobby was bright and modern. The receptionist smiled at him and asked, "Are you Bob Smith?"

Bob looked surprised and said, "Yes. Yes, I'm Bob Smith. How did you know?"

"We've been expecting you. I'll tell Craig that you're here. Please have a seat. Would you like a cup of coffee?"

"No, thank you, I'm fine for now." Bob sat down and tried to look at a magazine.

Moments later, a tall, casually dressed man came up to him. "Hi, Bob, I'm Craig Stevens. I'm glad to meet you. Why don't you come on back?" He led Bob through a series of winding hallways with an inordinate number of doors to a comfortable office with a nice view of downtown. "Please sit down. Make yourself comfortable. Would you like some coffee or a soft drink?"

"No thanks. I'm fine," Bob replied as he sat down at a small conference table. Craig picked up a pad, pen and cup of coffee off the desk and sat down at the table with Bob.

"So, how are you feeling?" Craig asked quietly.

"I'm fine, you?" Bob asked feeling a little puzzled.

"I'm fine, and thanks for asking," Craig said smiling. "But I want to know how you're really doing. You had a big shock yesterday. I expect that if you told your family last night, they were surprised too. You've been forced to think about things that I bet have not seriously crossed your mind in years. I want to know how you're dealing with that."

"Right now, I think I am fine, but that could change," Bob replied. "Over the last 24 hours I have been angry, scared, excited, depressed, panicked and overwhelmed. My wife cried, my daughter was worried about her social life, and on several occasions I've caught myself just sitting and staring – at nothing. You're right. This really wasn't something I expected, or had even considered. Maybe I should have seen it coming, but I didn't."

"That's okay. From what I understand from the Human Resources Director, very few people saw this coming. The company kept things very quiet. Well, one of the things I'm here for is to listen. So, as you start to feel your emotions changing, let's talk about it. The range of emotions is natural. When I meet with new clients, they describe a wide range of emotions when they received the news – ringing in their ears, blurred vision, feeling light-headed, nausea, and more. When they start thinking about telling their families – maybe having to relocate – they get a sense of panic and self-doubt.

"You will go through the stages of grieving. But, very quickly, you need to let go of any anger toward National Products or your circumstances. Holding on to that anger will be a huge barrier to your success and it will reflect in your communications with others, including potential employers. The last thing you want to share on a job interview is how poorly you feel you were treated by a former employer.

"Not to make this sound simple, but your situation is what it is. Maybe it could have been different, but it isn't. Being angry or burning bridges won't help you find a new job. You'll need all the positive energy you can muster to be successful."

Bob let this sink in. "I guess I understand what you're saying. I know I don't like to hear applicants complain about their old jobs or bosses. Okay, I'll work to keep myself positive and moving forward – but it won't always be easy."

"Of course it won't," Craig answered, "but it is important, and as you work through the process you'll see how much it will matter. Okay, let's start by you telling me all about yourself.

Give me the run down on your career, family history, everything."

Bob took a deep breath and started in. He worked from the beginning and his childhood growing up in Phillips, Indiana. They had a traditional middle-class life. Both of his parents worked. His father was a Professor, his mother a Librarian. They didn't have a lot, but they didn't know any better. He graduated from high school and went to college at a small private school not too far from home. He got good grades, worked a variety of part-time jobs and graduated with a degree in accounting. He got his first professional job as an accountant with a small manufacturing firm, Acme Manufacturing, here in Plainville. He thought about working on his CPA, but then talked himself out of it.

He met Linda while he was working at Acme. They caught each other's eye at a restaurant downtown over lunch. She was working as a secretary for a local art broker. They dated and eventually married. Now they have two kids and a house in the suburbs. While the house isn't huge, it is at the upper-edge of what he can afford.

After five years with Acme, a recruiter called him and told him about a job with National Products. He liked his job, but Amy had just been born and they needed a larger house. So he agreed to an interview and, to make a long story short, he took the job and never left. Over the last 15 years, he worked his way up to Section Manager in the Finance Department. He liked the company and the people he worked with. The pay was okay and the benefits were good. He had kind of assumed that he'd retire from National in another 20 years or so. So much for that idea.

Bob told Craig about his other activities: church, little league, etc. He felt like he was rambling, but just couldn't seem to stop. He glanced down at his watch and realized he had been talking for almost an hour. "Wow! I'm sorry. I guess I lost track of time. My throat's getting a little dry. I guess I could use that drink now."

Craig smiled again. "That's quite alright. I've learned a lot about you. Why don't we get that drink and I'll give you a quick tour of the place. Then we can come back and I'll tell you what I heard you say and what we've planned for the rest of your day."

Craig led the way to a bright, clean kitchen area. There was a refrigerator full of drinks, a coffee pot, and microwave. Some packages of cookies and crackers were on the counter. "Help yourself," Craig said as he refilled his coffee cup.

Bob picked up a Genesis Career Counseling coffee mug off the shelf and filled it. "This is very nice," he observed. "Where do I pay for this?"

"You don't." Craig answered. "We found out years ago that providing coffee, soft drinks and snacks does a lot for our clients' morale. We've found it helps people stay focused, which is what we're all about. What you'll find, Bob, is that looking for a job may be the most difficult job you've ever had. It's our responsibility to help keep you focused and to give you the tools and support you need to be successful. Let's go look around."

Craig and Bob walked through a seemingly maze of hallways and doors. Bob saw several small offices, just large enough for a desk and chair. On each desk was a phone and computer. About half the desks had someone working at them, while the others were empty and clean. Craig said Bob would be able to use any open office when he needed it.

They passed a large library full of corporate research materials and more computers. In the library were bulletin boards with job postings, advertisements for job fairs, and pictures of 'graduates' of the program. There was a small room with a video camera set up for practice interviews. Another room held a high quality copy machine and several large laser printers. There also was a large conference room with some pretty high-tech multi-media equipment that Craig said they used for training sessions and group meetings.

When they got back to Craig's office, Bob was thoroughly impressed. Craig had seen the look before. "Before you get the idea that this might be a good place to hang around, remind yourself that this is a good place to be while you're looking for a job. But your goal is to leave here, as quickly as possible, with a job that utilizes your skills and provides you with the income and career opportunity that you deserve. While this might look good now, in a few months you'll be glad to not be coming back.

"Let me tell you what I heard you say earlier." Craig continued. "While you didn't use these kinds of words, I heard you describe yourself as a hard-working, conscientious employee with a desire to help the company. You are a good family and community man with a comfortable, but not extravagant lifestyle. You have good self-confidence. You communicate well. You make good eye contact. All-in-all, I think you're going to be just fine.

"Let me give you an overview of the program here and then after lunch we'll get started. Our focus is to help you build the skills and give you the emotional support you need to find a new job. We'll help you work on your resume and practice 'telling your story.' We'll also work on your LinkedIn profile and talk about other ways to use social media. You and I will meet regularly, plus we'll have some 'group-therapy' sessions where you'll get together with some other clients to talk about career search techniques. Every Friday we have a meeting with all of our clients, where anyone can report on their progress that week, any job or company news they've picked up, and ask for help with any problems they've had.

"You have full access to all of the resources we saw on the tour. You can use a private office when you're making telephone calls or need some privacy. You'll be given access to the computer network so you can use the computers here and other research materials in the library. You also can work from home when you like – you can access all of our tools and resources online. You'll probably do most of your own word processing, but you can use our administrative assistants if your word processing skills need some work. And finally, you'll be surrounded by other people in the same boat you're in. I think you'll find that to be a good stimulant. You can share ideas and get encouragement. As I said earlier, you'll probably also develop a strong desire to get back to real work.

"Let me also help you set some expectations. This process will take time. I usually advise new clients to plan to search one month for every $10,000 of salary they expect to earn. So if you want a $40,000 a year job, plan on looking for four months. An $80,000 a year job might take eight months to find. That is not a hard and fast number, but the averages have been remarkably consistent. I don't want to depress you, but I also don't want you to expect to be back to work in two to three weeks."

Craig leaned back and smiled. "I know we've covered a lot, do you have any questions?"

Bob looked dazed. "Right now I have so many questions I don't know where to start."

Craig stood up. "That is perfectly understandable. Let me introduce you to a few people, and then you can go out and grab a bite of lunch. Let's plan on getting back together at 1:30 and get you settled in. Craig led Bob out of the office and introduced him around. He met the support staff, the IT Technician and the office Vice President. He learned that Genesis Career Counseling was a national organization and this was one of their 25 offices. With his head spinning, Bob left and drove off to find some lunch.

He bought a sandwich at a deli down the street and came back to his new "office." He wanted to explore a little before he met with Craig again. He was able to catch Stacy, the IT Technician, and she showed him how to log onto the computer network and access the Internet. The computers were loaded with current versions of common business software. The Internet connection was fast, and Bob went to a couple of his favorite sites, just to test drive the system. Finally, he slipped into one of the private offices and called over to National Products.

First he talked with Alice and arranged to come by late Friday afternoon to clean out his desk and say a few good-byes. Next he called Susan Johnston to get the real scoop on yesterday's announcement. Susan told him that there had been a big shakeup. Over 50 positions had been eliminated, some as high as Vice Presidents. There were several from accounting, including Bob and Frank Simmons. She had in fact received a slight increase in duties, and in pay, but not much. She was now reporting directly to Alice and had a little more supervisory responsibility over some of the accounting clerks. Things had been strange this morning, but they seemed to be calming down. They both agreed to spend some time catching up tomorrow afternoon when Bob cleaned out his office.

At 1:30 Bob went back to Craig's office. He told Craig about exploring the office and that he was feeling better about the facilities. He also told him that he had learned more about the changes at National Products. In hindsight, maybe a good severance package and outplacement assistance wasn't so bad. It sounded like others hadn't been so lucky.

Craig then gave Bob some "homework" for that afternoon and Friday. There was a skills profile test and a career interest survey to complete, along with URLs for a couple of online personality profiles. He also gave Bob a book of sample resumes and told him to take his first shot at putting one together. They would meet on Monday morning and start hitting the process hard.

As Bob walked back to his car, his mind was reeling again, but this time with good ideas. While he had only been in outplacement for less than a day, he was more confident that this was a good idea. He would be able to find a new job and get on with his life. He was starting to believe what he had been telling everyone else – it would be okay.

Friday afternoon Bob went back to National Products and cleaned out his desk. As he packed, he talked with Susan Johnston. They talked about the RIF and the impact on the company. It was evident to Bob, even in his brief goodbye conversations with his staff, that many people had been shaken by the news. Several employees told him, "If you find a good place and need someone, give me a call." It was clear that National Products would be feeling the effects of this reorganization for some time.

Walking out with his last box full of books and mementos was the hardest part. Some of his bitterness returned, but there was also a strong mixture of sadness. He had been coming to this building, and working with many of these people for a long time. He had known some of his co-workers for almost as long as he had known his wife. Leaving them behind wasn't going to be easy. On top of that, he worried some for National Products. He hoped the company would rebound from their problems and that his friends' jobs would be secure. Hopefully this reorganization wasn't the beginning of more serious problems.

That night Bob and Linda invited some old friends over for dinner. They had known Don and Jill Howell for years. Don and Bob had been best friends since high school. They sat on the deck, drank a few beers, and talked about Bob's pending career change late into the night. It felt good to confide in someone and Bob enjoyed the conversation. Don was a good and sympathetic listener. Having lost his job once before in a similar fashion, he was able to encourage Bob that things would work out and probably for the better.

I'm Fired?!?

Sunday morning Bob announced his situation to their Sunday school class. As the number of people that knew what was going on grew, his comfort level grew. Several people in class mentioned times they had also been RIFed. He felt more connected and less alone. That afternoon he worked on his resume some more and completed the assessments, and on Monday morning he was ready to begin his search in earnest.

CHAPTER 5 – NETWORKING 101

When Craig said "hit it hard" on Monday, he meant it. The day started promptly at 8 o'clock with a fast-paced meeting with Craig. After a brief discussion about their respective weekends and Bob's progress of telling his friends, Craig got down to business.

"Bob, before we begin the process, I want to make sure you understand our focus and strategy. Make no mistake; Genesis Career Counselors is not going to find you a job. We are not going to represent you to companies. We are not going to knock on doors for you. We are not going to negotiate for you. What we are going to do is teach you how to do those things for yourself. Over the next week or two we'll do quite a bit of training. We'll help you evaluate your career interests and put together a career search plan. After that, we'll help you execute your plan. I'll be here to give you feedback and encouragement, but beyond that, this is your job. The harder you work the process, the better the process will work for you. Like I told you last week, looking for a job is a full-time job, and it may be one of the hardest jobs you've ever done.

"There are two faces to the job market – the public face and the private face. The public face is represented by help-wanted ads and Internet job postings. This is the side that we find most of our clients are familiar with when they get here, and it's where they want to spend their time."

"That's what I was expecting," said Bob. "Don't I just post my resume on Monster.com or CareerBuilder, and then do some follow up? I assumed you would help me with that."

"Well, we will help you with that type of activity, but there is much more to it than that. Only about 25-30 percent of jobs are filled through the public side of the job market. You do need to be active there, but the key is to tap into the private side of the market."

Craig continued, "But before we jump into the private side, let's talk about what you are more familiar with. The Internet will be a huge resource for you in your search. You can learn incredible amounts of information about companies, you can find jobs, you can apply for jobs and you can use it to distribute your resume."

"I saw that!" Bob exclaimed. "Over the weekend I was looking at some sites. They said I could post my resume and that thousands of companies would have access to it. Shouldn't I do that right away – at least as soon as you help me with my resume?"

"Actually, Bob, we are not big fans of posting your resume on job boards."

Bob was puzzled, "Why not?"

"There are a couple of reasons. First, when you post your resume, you lose control of the job search. You don't know who looks at your resume, what position they are trying to fill or what context they have about you or your former employers. They also don't have any idea if you would be interested in the job they are trying to fill, or what specific skills you may or may not have, that would make you successful in that job.

"Secondly, when you post on job boards, you lose control of what your resume looks like. Frequently these boards have questions you answer to build their database, which is easily searchable, but is not easily displayed. When a recruiter prints your resume from these databases and hands it to a hiring manager, the resume is often difficult to read, and it does not represent you in the manner you want to be represented."

"So should I just avoid these job boards?" Bob asked.

"Absolutely not," answered Craig. "These boards are the primary face of the public job market. Internet job advertising has replaced newspaper advertising as the place companies turn first to get the word out. You'll want to check every board you can find on a regular basis to be aware of job opportunities. You'll also want to watch the newspapers closely. Remember, a good number of jobs are filled through this public part of the job program. As we get deeper into your training, we'll talk more about how to do the best searches on job boards, and how to use the Internet to your advantage.

"Let's shift to the private face of the market. The heart of our program is networking. Are you familiar with the concept?"

Bob thought for a moment. "I've heard the word before. It has always sounded kind of sleazy to me – like using people – the good-old-boy network – you know, it's not what you know but who you know. I don't know if I'd feel comfortable doing that." Bob squirmed a little as he thought about this.

"Some people view networking much like you do, and some use it like that," Craig explained. "But that is not what we're talking about. When we talk about networking at Genesis, we are talking about building a network, a framework if you will, of business contacts. Your objective will be to make sure that as many people as possible know about you, your background and what you are looking for. The broader we can make your network, the more likely that someone will have an opening that fits you."

As Craig talked, Bob took a few notes. (Figure 1) "Can't I just look in the job postings and work from there?" Bob asked.

"Sure you can," said Craig. "If you're in no hurry and aren't interested in the best jobs. Remember, the statistics show that less than one-third of jobs are filled from help-wanted advertisements. The other two-thirds are filled by other means, primarily personal contact. One person has a job to fill and someone else knows a person who could fill it. They meet and it happens. There is nothing shady or manipulative about it. This isn't the boys in the back room smoking cigars and helping out their friends. It's how businesses fill jobs."

Craig continued. "You'll start by making a list of everyone you know. These will form the start of your network. You'll also develop a target list of companies that you might want to work for. The target list is one of the most important networking tools you'll have. Companies on this list don't necessarily have to have open positions; they are just companies you want to know more about. This list will be a great conversation starter in many of your networking meetings.

"When your lists are ready, then you'll hit the phones and the street, and try to meet with everyone on your list. We suggest

	Networking Notes
	1) List <u>everyone</u> I know – not just those I think can help me
	2) Learn to say "Can you help me?"
	3) Use the A-I-R process:
	Advice – Information – Referral
	4) Tell my story
	5) Use referrals as door-openers
	6) Follow up on every referral
	7) Give feedback to everyone
	8) Use a target list to generate referrals
	9) Thank everyone who helped me

(Figure 1)

you tell them about your career background and goals and then use the A-I-R process, Advice – Information – Referral. You'll ask if they have any advice for your job search; you'll ask for information about their company; and then you'll ask if there is anyone they can refer you to.

"People are honored when you ask them for advice, so the A-I-R process starts there. By asking for advice about your job search, you are showing that you respect them, and I bet you'll be surprised about how many people you meet that will have been through just what you are going through now. Those people will give you tips and suggestions based on what worked for them. I think you'll find many of those ideas very helpful.

"Then you turn the conversation to them. Learn more about their company and how their career path led them to their current position. This personal information will help you connect with them. It also will help you put their earlier suggestions into context, which will help you use those ideas more effectively.

"Finally, you'll ask for referrals. It will be important to stress that you are not asking for names of people who currently have job openings – you are only asking for names of people, just like them, who would be willing to meet with you and help you expand your network. If they should say they can't think of anyone, then you'll use your target list and ask if they know anyone at these companies. Usually you'll walk out with two or three more names for you to contact. Your network will grow and grow."

"Do all of these networking meetings need to be face-to-face?" Bob asked. "That sounds like a lot of meetings."

Craig smiled. "It can be a lot of meetings; and, no, not all meetings will be face-to-face, but you'll find that personal contact will improve the chances for a successful meeting. Be flexible and be willing to meet them wherever it works best for them, in their office, over breakfast or coffee, or someplace else.

If they can't meet, ask if you can email them a copy of your target list and then call them back for a brief networking meeting over the phone.

"You'll follow the same time process online using LinkedIn and other business-oriented social networking sites. Your initial goal is to make contact with as many people as you can and to build your network. Social media can be very helpful in your search. Do you have a LinkedIn profile?"

"Kind of," Bob said with a shrug. "I set it up a while back, but I didn't put much energy into it, and I only have a few connections."

"How about a Facebook page?" asked Craig.

"About the same -- I have one but I don't use it very much."

Craig smiled. "You're in the same boat as most of our clients when they start with us. We'll help you update both of those. Let's start with Facebook. It tends to be a great place to connect with family and friends. It's a good way to tell people about your status and to keep them posted on your job search. The one issue with Facebook is that many people tend to tell a little too much online. You want this site to reflect the 'professional' Bob Smith so make sure you're not posting photos of wild parties or inappropriate activity."

"No worries," said Bob with a smile. "My wild side is pretty tame. Should I be trying to "Friend" more people?" Bob started taking some notes on social Networking. (Figure 2)

"Sure," Craig answered, "we want you to reach out to as many people as you can. Even connecting with your old high school and college classmates might open some doors for you. The other site we want you to focus on is LinkedIn. LinkedIn is

Social Media Notes

1) Use Facebook to communicate with family and friends
2) Make sure pages and photos are professional and business appropriate
3) Update LinkedIn profile to match resume
4) Use LinkedIn to:
   a) Communicate who I am and what I've done
   b) Research other companies
   c) Look for job openings
5) Join and be active in groups that match my experience and interests
6) Post new updates regularly

(Figure 2)

the largest and most successful business networking site and can be a great help to your search. There are at least three ways LinkedIn can help.

"First, like Facebook, it's a great way to tell your story and let people know you're available. You'll want to make sure your profile is complete and presents the right look for you. You'll want to make all the connections you can and you'll want to solicit recommendations from people you've worked with. You'll also want to join and be active in several groups that fit your interests and experience.

"Next, LinkedIn is a great way to research the market. You can use the system, as well as your connections, to find out more about the companies you might want to work for. Finally, LinkedIn is being used more and more by recruiters. They are posting their job openings on LinkedIn and combing the database for people to hire. We want you to be as visible as possible."

"I had no idea," said Bob. "What about Twitter or that insta-whatever-it-is?"

"At this stage, we don't use Twitter or Instagram as part of our networking process. They are great tools, but unless you are already familiar with them, we'll focus on Facebook and LinkedIn. If you want to tweet and those are tools you use already, we're happy to help you find better ways to use them. We've had clients use blogs and other tools to help spread their message."

"I guess I thought social media was just 'social' and not 'business'."

"Business is big on social media, Bob. Now, eventually, one of two things will happen. Either you'll meet someone who says something like, 'As a matter of fact, our Controller just resigned yesterday,' and you'll be in a position to interview for that job.

Or, some company will be talking about filling a job and someone will remember you and say, 'What about that Bob Smith guy I talked to last week? He'd be perfect for this job.' Then they give you a call and it goes from there.

"There are three keys to making networking work. The first is that you ask for help. As you meet with people, you need to use these four words: 'Can you help me?' People are generally good natured, and when you use those magic words, they will try to help you. But, if you don't ask for help and instead just wait for them to volunteer, you may be waiting for a long time. Similarly, you want to say 'I don't expect you to have a job for me.' This helps people relax because they won't have to tell you 'no.'

"The second rule is that you have to work the system. If someone gives you three referrals, you need to call those three people. You need to send thank-you letters or emails, and keep in touch with everyone you talk to. If your only contact with someone is one quick meeting, they will be less likely to help you in the future. But if you also contact the referrals they give you and give them feedback about your progress, the benefits of the network can increase dramatically.

"Finally, you have to give what you get. Networking is a two-way street. After you get a new job – and you will – people that you have networked with will call you or refer others to you. You've got to be willing to take the time, have the meetings, and give out names. If you'll do this, the cycle will continue."

Craig smiled and then continued, "One more thing about networking, you're going to need to check your ego at the door."

"I'm not sure I know what you mean," Bob said with a confused look on his face.

"Networking means asking for help. Some clients, particularly men, have trouble with that. For their entire lives, they've been taught to be self-reliant and independent. Our culture talks about pulling yourself up by your bootstraps. Now, I'm asking them to humble themselves and ask everyone they come in contact with for help. For some clients, this is a challenge they simply cannot overcome. But from what I've seen of you, we'll be able to work through any ego issues."

"I can see the challenges you're talking about. Thanks for warning me."

"Now, here is your schedule for the rest of this morning," Craig continued. "You've got an appointment at 9 o'clock in the Assessment Center where you'll go over the results of the tests you took over the weekend. They may also ask you to take some pen-and-paper career assessments. After that, you'll meet Rhonda, our resume specialist. She also will get you started on your target list. Sometime this morning, I expect that June, the facility coordinator, will track you down and help you get settled with a storage locker, supplies and telephone training. Any questions?"

Bob was feeling overwhelmed again. "No. I think I understand. Which way is the Assessment Center again?" Craig pointed the way and Bob officially started down the path to finding a new job.

Chapter 6 – Putting It In Writing

Step one was a visit with Rhonda the 'resume specialist'. After some glad-to-meet-you chatter, Rhonda dove in. "Bob, before I even look at your resume, the first thing I tell everyone is to be honest. In the long run you will not benefit by lying or exaggerating your credentials. That doesn't mean that you have to practice 'full disclosure' and tell everyone everything. But it does mean that you should not, for example, list a degree you haven't earned or a job you haven't held."

"No worries there," said Bob. "This is all factual. I have always been shocked when I hear about people who do that."

"Wonderful," said Rhonda, "now let's see what you've done." Rhonda looked over Bob's drafts and made some suggestions while he took notes (Figure 3). His biggest challenge would be making his resume reflect his personality – rather than look like the templates that he had used. "What you are striving for," Rhonda explained, "is a clean and clear way to tell your story. Readers need to know the facts about where you worked and what you did, but also who you are. Show them what makes you different from every other applicant they see. Help them understand how you can benefit their organization."

"Why did you cross out my Career Objectives section?" Bob asked.

Resume Notes

1) Be honest – falsifying a resume is a bad way to get a job

2) Express myself – make this a personal document

3) Clean and easy to read

4) Highlight accomplishments – 5-10 – and vary the list depending on the job I am applying for

5) Focus on enablers – avoid limiters

6) Avoid information not related to job (hobbies, health, marital status)

7) White or light colored paper

8) Use a similar format for letterhead

9) References and Salary History as separate document with similar style
   – supply only when requested

	10) For applying online, have PDF and plain-text versions available

(Figure 3)

"First, a recruiter is going to review your resume because you've expressed an interest in a position they are trying to fill. Therefore, your objective is obviously to get that job. To be blunt, at that stage of the review process the recruiter really doesn't care what you want. What they care about is filling their opening," Rhonda answered. "So, a two- or three-line summary of your skills and experience will be more helpful to them than what your career interests are. Now, I say that to you because you have some great experience. If you were a new college graduate without much experience, a career objective would be more appropriate.

"That makes sense," said Bob. "Tell me more about the accomplishments section you just inserted."

"Rather than listing the responsibilities of each job, like you have, I suggest you work on a series of bullet point items that showcase what you have accomplished in your career. A recruiter is less interested in what you were responsible for than what you accomplished. For example, listing that you reduced your operating costs by 30 percent through improved efficiencies is much more interesting than hearing that you oversaw the capital expense budget. Similarly, someone who can show they consistently met their performance objectives is more interesting than someone who can simply say they had difficult objectives. Also, quantify everything you can because numbers tell a great story. The accomplishment tells much more about you than the responsibility does."

"How many accomplishments should I list?"

"There is no magic number, but I would suggest you have less than 10. The real key is that you vary them depending on what job you are applying for. You should use different accomplishments based on the job and order them so the most relevant are listed first."

"I'm following you," said Bob. "How long should my resume be?"

"Lots of people seem hung up on the one page rule. My suggestion is that the length of your resume should be directly related to the length of your career; the longer your career, the longer your resume. In very few cases, however, do I suggest someone have a resume longer than two pages. As you build your resume, you need to think like a recruiter. They are trying to decide as quickly as possible if you are qualified for the job they are trying to fill. You need to assume they will not read your entire resume, but that they'll stop as soon as they think they have enough information to make that first yes/no decision. You need to organize your resume so the most important information is at the top. That is where a great summary comes into play. Then, if you've got strong accomplishments, list them next. A recent college graduate might not have much experience, so they are selling their education. In those cases, education needs to be close to the top. It's all about making the document sell you, as you need to be sold, and that is different for every job seeker.

"One more thing," Rhonda added, "in all aspects of your resume, focus on 'enablers' and avoid 'limiters'."

"Sorry," said Bob, "I have no idea what you are talking about."

Rhonda smiled. "You want this document to cause someone to want to talk with you. You want it to open doors. Enablers are words and phrases that make them want to learn more. They are positive, action-oriented words and phrases and help to show how you can help their company. Limiters are just the opposite. Limiters give the recruiter a reason to put your resume in the discard pile. For instance, an accomplishment that talked about you saving a prior company $500,000 would be an enabler. That is a good story, and a recruiter would want to learn more. An accomplishment where you only saved $50 might be a limiter. The recruiter could interpret this as mediocre performance.

"Next, put work-related information on your resume. Some people list hobbies, marital status, and other personal items. Our feeling is that all of these could be limiters and are rarely enablers. For example, let's say that one of your hobbies is golf. While it's possible the recruiter also plays golf and he'll be attracted to you because of that, it's also possible that the recruiter hates golf and thinks it's a waste of time. You run the risk that he'll discard your resume just because he thinks you'll spend more time on the golf course than at work. Being a good golfer won't help you land many accounting jobs so I think it's best to leave that kind of non-work-related information off your resume."

"Okay," said Bob, "it feels like it's all coming together. What kind of paper should I use, and what about online resumes?"

"At Genesis, we strongly encourage you to use a high-quality white paper. If you think another color better represents you, that's your choice. One thing to keep in mind is how well your resume will copy. Sometimes darker colors of paper won't copy or fax well, and you have to be prepared that the resume you leave with a company might be faxed or scanned. As for the online resume, you need to be ready with several versions. We suggest that when you can, you submit your resume in a PDF format. This can be read by all recipients, but it can't be altered. It also does not require the company to use the same word processing software or have the same fonts that you have. There are a number of free applications that will convert your document to a PDF."

"Stop right there," said Bob. "Speaking of fonts, does that really matter?"

"To a degree it does. We suggest you pick one fairly standard font and use it for your resume and all of your other printed materials. You do not have to use Times or Arial, but whatever you choose should be clean and easy to read. Multiple fonts, or very unique fonts, can be distracting. Only individuals looking for creative or artistic positions should use artwork or highly original layouts or fonts. Most of our clients are better served by using a more standard and professional look.

"You also need to be prepared to submit a resume online where they will ask you to copy and paste your resume into their applicant tracking system. These systems will often strip out all formatting and use a plain-text format. You should be prepared with a plain-text version of your resume. This way you will be able to control the spacing and formatting more so than if you simply try to paste in your normal word processing version."

"Writing a resume is a lot harder than I thought," said Bob. "Thank you for all the pointers. One quick question about thank-you letters; do you recommend real letters or emails?"

"Again, part of the answer depends on you and how formal you like to communicate. Email is less formal than letters. Hand-written notes are more personal than typed notes. The 'right' communication depends on a mix of your style and the situation. As a general rule, email is fine for pre-approach messages where you are asking for an appointment. Email is also fine for follow-up communications and as thank-you notes for networking meetings. These are all less formal communications. We suggest you send paper thank-you notes for job interviews. You can type those or send hand-written notes based on your personal style."

"With my hand-writing, I think I better stick to typing," laughed Bob. "Do you have any suggestions about how to apply for jobs I see posted in the newspaper or online?"

"Another good question," Rhonda replied. "The first rule is to follow the company's rules. If they ask for resumes to be submitted online, then submit yours online. If they ask you some qualifying questions, then answer those questions honestly and as completely as you can. If they need a paper application filled out, then fill it out completely. Not following the process the company has implemented can be a real limiter.

"But don't stop there. Before you apply, find out as much as you can about the company and the position. Try to find out who the hiring manager is. LinkedIn can be a great source for that kind of information. Make sure that your resume and cover letter reflect how you meet the job requirements. Point out how you can help their company to be even more successful. Then, after you've applied the way HR wants you to, send your resume with a cover letter directly to the hiring manager. We've found that often the recruiter is swamped with work and your resume might get lost in the pile. But, if the hiring manager is interested, your likelihood of an interview goes up dramatically.

"Also, once you have your resume in shape, you should use that same format and language to update your LinkedIn profile. Our goal is to make sure you are presented in a consistent and professional fashion. Anytime someone asks about Bob Smith, we want them to get the same answers and to see a consistent image.

"And one last thing," Ronda added, "we'll help you make up some simple business cards. Nothing fancy, but with a look consistent with your resume and other documents. These are very helpful at networking events or job clubs where you aren't passing out resumes but want to exchange contact information."

"Great suggestions," said Bob, "this is just what I needed."

By noon, in addition to meeting with Craig and Rhonda, Bob had taken two more career interest assessments tests, been assigned a storage locker, learned how to use the phone system, copier and fax machine, and met some other outplacement clients.

I'm Fired?!?

Several of the other clients were from National Products. The one Bob was most surprised to see was Frank Simmons. Simmons still had a very negative attitude about his entire experience and frequently complained loudly both about his separation and the services provided by Genesis Career Counseling.

Apparently Frank had met with Alice shortly before Bob had. That explained some of the stress Alice had shown. Frank boasted that he "told Alice and National Products what they could do with their reorganization."

Like Bob, he had gone in that Friday and cleaned out his desk. Unlike Bob, he had not yet told his wife or his friends (if he had any, Bob thought).

"I don't want to worry her," Frank said. "She doesn't handle this type of thing well. So, I figure I'll come in here every day while these guys find me a new job. When they find me one, then I'll tell Mildred and the kids."

"Don't you think they'll catch on?" Bob asked. He was stunned. He couldn't imagine keeping this type of secret from Linda. "What happens if they call the office or if they talk with someone else from work?"

"Don't worry about it. I told them that Alice was yelling at me for too many personal phone calls and not to call me. Plus, Mildred's not too bright. She'll never catch on." Frank laughed. "Besides, what's she going to do if she finds out? Leave me? Fat chance of that." He chuckled to himself as he walked off to the kitchen area. Apparently, since Frank found out that he didn't have to pay for soft drinks or snacks, he was making sure he got his fair share.

"I guess he didn't get the same networking speech that I got." Bob mumbled to himself.

Making a target list was more work than Bob thought it would be. He used the notes he'd taken while meeting with Rhonda (figure 4). He was trying to develop a list of 15 to 20 companies that he thought he might like to work for. They weren't companies that necessarily had openings – they were just prospects. He would use the list during networking meetings to help the people he was meeting with think of names to refer him to. As he found out more about the companies on the list, he would move them up or down the priority list, or drop them and add others.

He was using a variety of research materials to compile his list. Genesis had several commercial directories for this purpose. He also was doing research on the Internet and using LinkedIn. Bob and Craig agreed that based on his career assessments and his experience, his first assault on the job market should be to identify jobs similar to the one he just left. He included the larger manufacturing companies in the area as well as a couple of service firms. While he didn't know much about those industries, he knew that they were good companies and his skills should be very transferable. If he was going to change companies, he might as well work someplace that treated their employees well.

Target List Notes

1) Pick 15 – 20 companies
2) With or without known job openings
3) Vary the size and industry
4) Include companies I know I'd like to work for and others I'm not sure about
5) Use as prompt, if network contact has no referral suggestions
6) Add or delete companies as I find out more about them

(Figure 4)

Chapter 7 – Blowing Your Own Horn

That afternoon Bob had his first interview training. Stacy Rodney was Genesis' Interviewing Trainer. She had many years of experience as a recruiter and knew all the tricks of the trade. It was her job to get Genesis' clients ready for their interviews. She told Bob that she would help him get ready for networking interviews, job interviews and eventually for the negotiation discussions that would happen toward the end of his search.

After introductions and some small talk, Stacy began. "Bob, the majority of this first training session will be a few practice interviews. I'll ask you questions and you'll answer them. After the interview we'll talk about what went well and what we need to work on. The third time we go through this we'll video tape the interview. With that tool we'll start working as much on how you interview as what you say.

"Before we start, I want to give you a few tips to keep in the back of your mind. First, an interview is simply a conversation. It is not life or death. You don't need, or want, to get hired for every job you interview for. So just relax. Be yourself. From what I see and understand, you have a good story to tell. Just calmly tell it. Look the interviewer in the eye, take your time, speak slowly and clearly, but not so slowly that you sound boring or uncertain. Be prepared – know who you are interviewing with and as much as possible about the company and the position before the interview starts. Have some questions ready and don't be afraid to ask them. Don't focus your questions on what the company can do for you, but on how you'll be able to help the company.

"Avoid food and drinks. They are simply opportunities for you to spill something or otherwise distract yourself or the interviewer. At the same time, don't appear unsociable or rude. If they press you, take the drink, but don't drink much. Dress appropriately. Try to dress just a little better than you would dress if you worked there. Don't wear a suit if the interviewer is in a golf shirt. Don't wear just a shirt and tie if the interviewer is wearing a suit. Do your research about the company and dress appropriately.

"Take at least two clean copies of your resume with you to every interview, even if you have already supplied it. One of our staff suggests taking five copies, but I'm okay with taking at least two. Take something to write on, and take notes about the job and the company." Stacy looked at Bob. It looked like she was trying to read his mind. "I think you're ready, so let's give it a try. Since you haven't had time to do much research, let's pretend that you are interviewing for your old job. I'll be a recruiter in the Human Resources department with National Products. Why don't you step outside, knock on the door, and we'll walk through one."

Bob left the office and closed the door. He felt a little silly standing in front of a closed door, but he remembered how important they told him role playing was. Taking a deep breath, he knocked and Stacy welcomed him to the Human Resources offices of National Products. After a 30-minute interview they sat back and critiqued the training session.

"Overall, Bob," Stacy summarized, "you did a good job. You appeared comfortable and relaxed. You looked me in the eye and spoke clearly. You have a habit of tapping your pen. You'll have to be careful about that. It may really annoy some people. What did you think?"

Bob considered the question. "It was okay, I guess. I was probably more relaxed because I knew it was just a training session, but I still felt nervous. I hated those questions you asked about 'what is my greatest strength' and 'what are my weaknesses'. I feel like I am blowing my own horn and I don't really like to do that. I also don't like telling someone else what I'm not good at."

"Those are two very common questions that you'll need to get used to answering. I personally don't think they are good interview questions, but a lot of interviewers will ask them. As far as blowing your own horn, blow it. Did you ever play in a band, maybe in high school?"

"Yeah, I played the trumpet." Bob smiled as he remembered. He had really enjoyed band class.

"Good," Stacy responded. "Do you remember what happened if you didn't blow hard enough?"

"Sure, the sound was weak and it was difficult to hold the note so the tone wavered," said Bob.

"Okay, what happened if you blew too hard?

"Just the opposite. The note would come out harsh. It sounded really bad."

"Exactly!" Stacy clapped her hands together. "Interviewing is blowing your own horn, and it's just like playing your trumpet. If you don't blow your own horn, nobody else will and it will just lay there and not make a sound. If you blow it too softly it will be difficult for people to hear your message and they may have trouble understanding it. If you blow it too hard you'll overwhelm your audience and they won't like what they hear. You have to blow your own horn with confidence and balance. If you do, you'll have better interviews and you'll get more job offers."

Bob liked analogies and saw how this one would help him. This training was really going to help.

"Now, about your weaknesses," Stacy continued, "nobody is perfect. We can all improve on at least one character trait. You probably know what yours is, but if not, over time, I'll try to help you find it. The key to the interview is to present this weakness in a positive light. Don't focus on what you do wrong; focus on how you are working to improve. Or, talk about how that weakness may actually have a benefit for others."

"I'm not sure I follow you there." Bob said.

"For example, if someone asks me what my weaknesses are, I say patience. I am not a very patient person. But, what that means is that I can also be described as driven. I like to get things done. I don't like to wait on others. I don't let things just sit and be unnecessarily delayed. While my lack of patience may get me in trouble sometimes, especially with my husband and my kids, I can transform a lack of patience into a sense of urgency which is something companies like.

"When you answer that question you don't have to give a laundry list of all your faults and failings. If you can find one or two things that you know you'd like to improve and then find the positive side of that 'failing,' you'll be able to sail through that part of the interview." After their second practice interview Stacy gave Bob several papers. "Here is a list of commonly asked interview questions. Bob, you'll notice that a lot of these questions are behaviorally based questions – those that start with 'tell me about a time when …'. Behaviorally based interviewing is a great way to evaluate a candidate. The theory is that past behavior is the best predictor of future actions. When someone asks you to tell them how you would handle a certain situation, you'll probably tell them what you think they want to hear. Since this is a hypothetical question, you can give the ideal answer. But, if instead they ask you to tell them about how you handled that type of situation in the past, you will probably tell them a real story and the odds are, that's how you'll handle that situation the next time it comes up.

"To answer behavioral based questions, we want you to use the C-A-R approach – Challenge, Action, Result. Start with describing what the challenge was you were facing or the problem you were trying to solve. Then tell them about the actions that you took. Finally, talk about the results you achieved. Using these three steps will help you make sure to tell the full story and keep everything in context.

"Sometimes these questions can be challenging. Take your time to think about a good response to the question. A good interviewer will be able to stand the silence and give you the time you need.

"Now, your homework before our next session is to sit down and write out an answer for each of these questions. Don't just think about them; really write down your answers. The mechanics of writing will help you clarify your thoughts and you'll get better answers. Then, practice saying your answers aloud two or three times each. In a few days we'll have another practice interview, this time with video tape, and see how much you've improved."

Bob spent the rest of the afternoon and the following morning reviewing his notes (figure 5) and doing his homework. He wrote answers to the questions, practiced his responses, worked on his target list and finished his resume – again.

He felt like things were starting to come together. His next training session with Stacy went even better. He was much more confident answering her questions. He even fielded some surprise questions pretty well. By looking at the video tape, he became aware of how he was sitting and his facial expressions. He also noticed that he was still tapping his pen. On the second run through, he did even better and felt like he was ready to start talking to people.

Interviewing Notes

1) Relax – be myself
2) Be prepared – know about the company and the interviewer
3) Dress one step above daily work clothes
4) Avoid drinks and food (but don't be unsociable)
5) Speak slowly and clearly
6) Use the C-A-R approach – Challenge, Action, Result
7) Keep answers focused
8) Make eye contact
9) Take notes
10) Ask questions

(Figure 5)

CHAPTER 8 – TELLING THE TALE

"Mr. Stanton will see you now." The Assistant smiled and led Bob in to see Gus Stanton, Vice President of Finance and CFO for Warner Industries. Bob had been referred to Mr. Stanton by his friend, Don. This was his first networking meeting and he was more than a little nervous.

Bob had spent the rest of his first week making phone calls and setting up meetings. Craig had warned him that some people he called might have someone screening their calls. If this happened, Bob would need to make it clear that he was calling for personal reasons and not trying to sell anything. Asking the Assistant for help by sending the call through could be very effective. He tried this and the call sailed through to Mr. Stanton. Bob had briefly explained that he was a friend of Don Howell and Don had suggested that Bob contact Mr. Stanton. He would just need ten or fifteen minutes of Mr. Stanton's time for a personal matter. Mr. Stanton said that he had some experience networking himself and he agreed to meet with Bob early the following week.

The office was large and comfortable. Mr. Stanton stood, shook Bob's hand, and offered him a seat across the desk.

"Well, Bob," Mr. Stanton started. "What can I do for you?"

Bob took a deep breath and launched into his well-rehearsed speech. "Mr. Stanton, as I mentioned on the phone, Don Howell is a long-time friend of mine and he said that you may be able to help me."

"Don's a good guy – plays a mean round of golf. If he thinks I can help you, then I'll do my best. What can I help you with?" Mr. Stanton replied with a smile.

"Well, for the last 15 years, I have held a variety of accounting positions with National Products. Most recently I was a manager in the Finance Department. I don't know if you've heard, but a few weeks ago they announced some fairly dramatic reorganization plans and they eliminated a level of management. Unfortunately, that level was my level. I am now 'available to industry' and looking for a job." Bob hoped that his humor would help break the ice. From the look on Mr. Stanton's face, it didn't work.

"I'm sorry, Bob, but we don't have any openings right now. If you'll leave a copy of your resume with my Assistant, I'll have it sent down to Human Resources. I'm sure that if something comes up they'll give you a call." Mr. Stanton had started to stand while saying this.

Bob's heart sunk. This wasn't going like it was supposed to. He quickly held up his hands. "No, no, no. Please, I didn't mean to ask you for a job. I wouldn't want to put you on the spot like that." Mr. Stanton sat back down. "I am trying to build a network of people that know me, and my background. If I can have ten to fifteen minutes I'd like to tell you about my experience and what I'm looking for. Maybe then you'll be able to suggest someone that I might call. I don't expect them to have an opening either. But the more people I talk to, the better the chances are that when something does open up, someone will remember our conversation and call me about the job."

Bob's heart stopped pounding as Mr. Stanton sat back and smiled. "I understand," he said. "Tell me your story and let's see where it takes us."

Bob pulled out a copy of his resume and briefly talked over the high points. He reviewed some of his major accomplishments and finally talked about his career search. "What I'd really like to find, is another manager of finance type job, in a manufacturing company. Maybe it's a Controller, or an Accounting Manager, or even Investments. I think my background in manufacturing is something I need to capitalize on."

Mr. Stanton asked a few questions to clarify some of Bob's experience and then sat back. "Well, Bob, it sounds like you are headed in the right direction. It's too bad we don't have any openings now. From this little conversation I think you might be a good addition to our team. I tell you what though, why don't you call…?" Mr. Stanton turned to his computer, opened Outlook and gave Bob the names and phone numbers of three other CFO's of manufacturing companies in the area.

The A-I-R model that Craig had taught Bob flashed through his mind. "Mr. Stanton, before we wrap up, I wonder if you could tell me a little more about Warner Industries – and about your career. I'd also like to know if you have any advice you might give me for my job search?" Mr. Stanton sat back, smiled, and told Bob his story.

"Mr. Stanton, this has been wonderful. Thank you for your time today and for these referrals. I will keep in touch with you and let you know how these develop. If things change here, or if you hear of anything else, I would appreciate it if you'd give me a call." Bob rose, shook Mr. Stanton's hand, and virtually floated out of the office. His first networking meeting had gone almost exactly as it should have. He now had three more good referrals to follow up on. He also had his resume in front of the decision maker at one of the companies on his target list. Maybe this wouldn't be so bad after all.

Back at "the office" as Bob now referred to Genesis, he met with Craig and Stacy and reviewed the meeting.

"Overall," Bob said with a smile, "I think it went really well. I wasn't too nervous, I learned some things about Warner Industries and I got three more referrals. I didn't trip on the carpet, sneeze on Mr. Stanton, or anything."

"That's great, Bob," said Craig. "I knew you'd be able to do it. Give us the full play-by-play."

They talked through the entire meeting with Craig and Stacy making minor suggestions. Bob hadn't used his target company list, but really hadn't needed to. He also didn't quite get the A-I-R in the right order, but he covered all the topics. They talked about several questions Mr. Stanton asked and how Bob could have answered them differently. They then looked at his schedule for the rest of the week.

"Well, Bob," Craig observed, "it looks like you are off to a great start. I'd like you to talk about this meeting at our group session on Friday. We've got a few other clients that aren't making the progress you are. Maybe your success will help motivate them. Also, you need to expand your contact list. I know you know more than the fifteen people you've written down."

"Sure I know more people than that." Bob was a little hurt by Craig's comment. "But I only listed those that I thought might know somebody. Why bother to list a bunch of people just to fill up the list?"

"Bob, you never know who knows who," Stacy jumped in. "We had a client once that got a lead on a job through a neighbor boy. The boy noticed the client sitting on his porch when he walked by on the way home from school and asked him why he wasn't at work. When the client mentioned that he was out of work, the boy said that at dinner the night before his father had been talking about having trouble hiring somebody. It turned out the boy's father was the president of a local company and was looking for a new Vice President. Our client made a networking call to the father, using his son as his introduction and wound up getting the job. He never would have expected a kid to be able to give him a networking referral, but he did. Don't underestimate the power of your network. Make it as big as you can. Remember – work the system and then let the system work for you."

Over the next several weeks Bob did just that. He averaged around ten to fifteen telephone calls each day to try to schedule networking meetings. From those calls, he was able to average five networking meetings each week. He polished up his LinkedIn profile and spent time finding and connecting with as many people as he could. Gradually his network grew. Keeping up with the thank-you letters, and the related corporate research was keeping him busy. He learned a lot about many different companies and made several updates to his target company list. Unfortunately, he hadn't heard of a single job opening that fit what he was looking for. His frustrations and concerns were beginning to grow again.

After about two months of "hitting it hard," Bob was getting tired. He was working on his fourth generation of networking and the quality of the contacts seemed to be dropping. He was scheduling fewer appointments and was getting fewer referrals with each meeting. To broaden his network, he began using some different techniques.

Going back to his target list, he began making cold-calls on the Chief Financial Officer at some of the companies. Much like a product salesman might do, he would simply walk into the lobby of the target company and try to get in to see the CFO. If he was successful, he gave his standard pitch. If the CFO was unavailable or was unwilling to see him, he would leave his resume and a prepared letter with the receptionist. The technique worked occasionally and he was able to gain some contacts.

He also used some pre-approach letters for some of his networking contacts that he felt were less likely to be successful. For these contacts he would send a letter or email describing his situation and telling them that he would be calling them in the following week. A week later he would call and use his letter as his opening, rather than a referral from another person. This seemed to increase his 'hit rate' and he scheduled more networking meetings. Sometimes he would include a resume in the initial letter and then do the networking over the phone.

While this was occasionally effective, the face-to-face meeting was still his best bet. He found that when he included the resume, sometimes his letter got shuffled off to HR and filed away, which didn't help with the networking meeting he was trying to arrange.

Linda was beginning to be more concerned. Even though Bob still had almost three months of pay remaining, the reality of looking for a job for over two months without a single real interview was concerning. Every night he gave her an update on his progress. He continued to work with Craig, Rhonda and Stacy to fine-tune his resume and his interviewing skills. They continued to encourage him to be patient – the right opportunity would come along if he just worked the system. Bob's attitude was still mostly positive, especially around the other Genesis clients, and he frequently offered help and shared his networking list with others.

Frank Simmons was a much larger concern to the staff of Genesis Career Consultants than Bob was. Even though Bob hadn't had any offers, he was continuing to work the system. Frank, on the other hand, was not. He claimed to be so uncomfortable with networking that he just wouldn't do it. Instead, he sent unsolicited resumes to seemingly every company in town. Frank would do the research of going through various directories to find the names and addresses of CFO's, Controllers and Accounting Managers. Then he'd fire off a resume and a generic cover letter. He also responded to virtually every help-wanted ad in the local papers or online, regardless of how well the job fit his qualifications. Unlike Bob, he did have a few interviews, but never more than one with any company.

As his frustration grew, so did his negative attitude. The other clients, and much of the staff, started avoiding Frank so they wouldn't have to listen to his whining and complaining.

Bob felt badly for Frank. Although he knew Frank's work history and work habits, he didn't want to see the guy be unemployed forever. Bob's family was concerned, but understanding and supportive. Frank's family was not. Two weeks prior, Frank's wife, who had just found out that Frank had been fired, came to Genesis and berated Frank's counselor for not finding him a job. Apparently their finances were not very stable and Frank's severance period had run out.

Then, one Thursday afternoon things changed. Bob was returning to Genesis after a networking meeting that had not gone well. The person he was meeting with kept him waiting in the lobby for over 45 minutes, and then only met with him for five minutes. Before Bob could even finish his story, the man stopped him and said that he didn't know why they were meeting. He said that he didn't have any accounting jobs open and didn't know who did. He abruptly stood up and showed Bob the door. The only good that seemed to come from that meeting was that Bob concluded that if this guy was an example of the managers with this firm, Bob could take that company off his target list. It was no place he wanted to work.

When he got back to the office, he had a telephone message from Stan Johnson. Stan was a CFO that Bob had networked with the prior week. Their meeting had gone okay, but not great. Stan had offered one referral name and been pleasant. Bob was surprised to see the message and called him back right away.

I'm Fired?!?

Stan said that his firm, Galaxy Construction, had just decided to create a new position called Accounts Payables Manager and would like to talk to Bob about the job. Bob's hopes skyrocketed! Trying to control his enthusiasm, Bob said that he was very interested in learning more about the job and they scheduled an interview for the following week.

There was hope, after all!

CHAPTER 9 – THE INTERVIEW

The weekend seemed to drag by. Bob spent much of his time researching Galaxy Construction and working on his interview preparation. By the time his interview came around, he felt as prepared as possible.

"Bob, good to see you again! Come on in." Stan Johnson was all smiles as he welcomed Bob into his office. "Thanks for coming in today. I'm really excited about this job and you just may be the guy we need."

"Thanks, Stan. I appreciate your confidence." Bob was a little surprised by Stan's excitement. They really hadn't spent much time together, but he wasn't about to complain. If Stan was that interested in Bob for this job, then Bob was interested too.

Stan was enthusiastic and jumped right into it. It seemed to Bob that Stan could hardly keep his seat. "Bob, I know we just met a couple of weeks ago and you did an excellent job of telling me about yourself, your experience and all that, so let me tell you more about this job. We are trying to implement a new accounting system and we're not sure that some of our people have the right stuff to get this project punched over the top. So, we want to bring in someone that's a hard charger – knows all about big company financial systems and knows how to manage other people. We've got some folks that, well, may not be the brightest bulbs in the box, if you know what I mean, and we need someone who can look over their shoulders and make sure they stay on the right track. Keep their noses to the grindstone – know what I mean? Now, I don't want to be talking out of school and putting bad ideas in your head, but we need someone who can come in and push this ball over the goal line. Based on our meeting awhile back, I think you may be the guy. What do you think about that?"

Bob didn't know what to think. What was this guy really talking about? 'Not the brightest bulbs in the box?' Was this any way to talk about your staff? But... it was a job – which was something that he needed. "Well, Stan, this sounds interesting. Can you tell me more about what you're looking for? What kinds of responsibilities are involved with 'pushing this ball over the goal line'?"

Stan looked a little taken aback. "Well, manager-type responsibilities. You've been a manager. You know. It's things like checking the clerks' work, making sure they didn't screw up. Watching their attendance. Training them in the way we do things. Keeping them on their toes. Making sure they aren't wasting time. Firing bad ones and hiring new ones. Cracking the whip. The usual kind of stuff. Are you interested?"

Bob's head was spinning, but, he kept telling himself, this is a job. I need to keep myself in the game, at least until I know what this guy is talking about. "Of course I am. What can you tell me about the department? How many employees, how many invoices, things like that?" Maybe he could get enough information to make sense of things.

"Good questions, good questions." Stan replied standing up. "Tell you what, I'm gonna let you spend some time with Steve Hamilton. Steve's our Controller and he can fill you in more about this job and anything else you want to know."

Stan quickly moved Bob out of his chair and down the hallway to a small and cluttered cubicle. A haggard looking man was just putting down his telephone. "Steve," Stan said, almost shouting, "I want you to meet Bob Smith. Bob is the guy I think we want to hire for that new manager position over in Payables. I want you to fill him in on the job and answer all of his questions."

Steve looked up, puzzled. "What new manager position in Payables?" he asked. "I thought we were just going to reorganize and have Sarah oversee the area. There's hardly enough volume to keep two clerks busy, what do we need a manager for?"

Bob could see this was an awkward situation and that Steve had been caught off guard. He wanted to just crawl out the door, but Stan would have none of it. Stan stepped closer to Steve. "I know that's what we talked about, but I brought our idea up to the Executive Committee and they didn't like my plan. Said something like they don't think Sarah could handle it or something. If we get the new customers we're talking about, we'll need someone with some whiskers and Bob here is the best we've seen. Now, we don't need to have this conversation right now, especially not in front of Bob here. You chat with him like I asked, and we'll get together later today and make sure we're all singin' off the same hymnbook." With that, Stan turned and walked back to his office, leaving Bob standing in the aisle and wishing there was a rock he could climb under.

"Okay," said Steve with a deep sigh, "let me clear off some space and you can sit down." He smiled weakly at Bob and moved a tall stack of papers off his guest chair. Bob sat down slowly. He must have looked like he was ready to bolt and Steve could sense it. "I'm sorry you had to see that. Stan's a pretty nice guy, usually, but sometimes he starts talking long before he's thought about what he's going to say. Things are a little crazy around here, and he kind of caught me by surprise, but that's not your fault, so let's try to start over." Steve took a long, slow breath and extended his right hand. "Hi, I'm Steve Hamilton."

Bob shook Steve's hand and smiled. "Nice to meet you, Steve. I'm Bob Smith." That simple act seemed to erase much of the tension and a good conversation followed. Steve told Bob a lot about Galaxy Construction and about Stan and the finance department. They talked about the staff, the planned expansion of accounts and the new system. Steve also asked a number of good questions about Bob's background and experience. The two had quite a bit in common and wound up talking for almost two hours about the company and their personal lives.

At about 4:30 Steve looked at the clock. "Wow! I didn't realize it had gotten so late. I'm sorry to have to wrap this up, but I've got some things I need to finish before I go home. I really enjoyed meeting you and getting to know you. I agree with Stan that I think you'd be a good addition to our team. I'll talk with Stan in the morning and we'll see what happens." He stood and walked Bob to the elevators.

Bob thanked Steve for his time and expressed his interest in the job. He drove home that afternoon replaying the conversations. Although Stan had seemed a little excitable, Steve seemed like a great guy to work with. Maybe this would work out after all.

The next afternoon, as Bob was working on thank-you letters to Stan and Steve, his telephone rang.

"Hello, this is Bob Smith." He answered.

"Bob, my name is Ron Peoples. I am the Vice President of Human Resources for Galaxy Construction. I understand you visited with some of our folks in finance yesterday."

Bob was instantly excited. "Yes. Yes, I had some very good conversations with Steve Hamilton and Stan Johnson yesterday. Do I need to schedule some time to speak with you?" Bob was already thinking job offer. He wondered how much salary they would offer him. He couldn't wait to finish this conversation and call Linda.

"No, Bob. I'm afraid there has been some confusion." Bob's heart sunk as Ron sighed deeply. "I apologize for all of this, but Stan didn't have the authority to contact you, nor to let you believe that we were going to create a new position. From what I understand from Steve, Stan virtually offered you a job. He shouldn't have done that. He knows the procedures better than that. He also knew that we needed to talk to him about some other issues."

Bob wasn't sure where this was headed, but he wanted to salvage this opportunity. He'd had a taste of success and wasn't about to let Human Resources 'procedures' get in his way. "I can understand how Stan might have gotten a little ahead of himself," he said. "If I need to wait awhile so you can get the administrative procedures caught up, that's no problem. What if I call Stan and offer to hang loose for a week or two? That will give him some time to get his ducks in a row and then we'll start over." Bob was pushing, but he wanted this job.

"Well, Bob," Ron said with another big sigh, "I'm afraid it's just not that easy. Unfortunately, Stan is no longer with Galaxy Construction. We've reorganized and his position was eliminated. We won't be creating a position called Accounts Payables Manager. I've looked at your resume and spoken with Steve Hamilton. You've got a good background and Steve seemed to like you, but you don't fit any of our current openings, or any we expect to have in the near future. Of course, we'll keep your resume on file and if things change we may give you a call. Once again, I'm sorry for the confusion and I wish you the best of luck in your search."

Before Bob could even respond, the line went dead. He dropped the phone back into its cradle and stared out the window. Just 30 seconds ago he was wondering how much money Galaxy Construction would offer him, and now he was left with 'don't call us, we'll call you.' He was back at ground zero.

Bob walked slowly to Craig's office and told him the story.

"I'm sorry to hear that, Bob." Craig was sincerely disappointed for Bob. They had met this morning and Bob had been bursting with excitement. "I know you are disappointed, but you'll be okay. At least you've had some interest now. You've gotten a couple of real interviews under your belt. And even though you didn't get this job, it wasn't because of you. It

I'm Fired?!?

sounds like they liked you. They just had a guy running a little out of control. That stuff happens. Why don't you go home today and relax? Play with the kids tonight and come back in the morning and get after it again."

Bob knew Craig was right, even if he didn't want to hear it. "Yeah, okay, I'll see you tomorrow."

On his way back to his desk, Bob saw Frank Simmons packing up some of his things. Even though he was in no mood to talk to Frank, he walked over to see what was going on.

"What's up, Frank?'

"I'm outta here, Buddy. That's what's up." Frank was visibly upset and virtually throwing files into his briefcase. "My old lady just called and said she's taking the kids and going to live with her mother. She says if I can't get a simple job then I'm not a man she wants her kids around. Doesn't she know they're my kids too? That witch. We'll see who kicks who in the pants in divorce court. If she thinks it's so darned easy to get a job, why doesn't she try it? Hasn't worked a day in her life. I'll tell you one thing. She ain't gettin' no alimony out of me, the witch!"

Bob stammered, trying to think of the right thing to say. "Gosh, Frank. I'm sorry," was all that came out.

"Not as sorry as she's gonna be, the witch!" Frank growled.

"Try to calm down, Frank. Why are you packing up your files?" Bob's mind was racing. Should he get Frank's counselor? How was he supposed to deal with this?

"I'm leaving, Bob. I already talked to Craig. This place ain't working for me. We've been here for weeks and, if you haven't noticed, we're still here. Neither one of us has even one good prospect and I'm out of severance. I've got to get a job today.

An old buddy of mine knows a guy who's looking for someone to work construction and that's what I'm gonna do. Leave this stupid accounting work to guys like you. I never did like it. See ya!" With that, Frank turned and marched out of the building.

Bob was speechless.

CHAPTER 10 – ON MY OWN

Two more months passed and a combination of fear and dread began to creep into Bob's life. Over those weeks he had continued to work his plan. He had now networked with over 100 people and sent letters and resumes to another 50 or so. He had responded to over 30 help wanted advertisements, he now had over 250 LinkedIn connections, and he was posting job search updates on his Facebook page.

Craig's early advice about ego crept back into Bob's subconscious. Sometimes when he talked with people, he felt embarrassed to say that he'd been out of work for months. His pride was hurt and he felt like he wasn't being an adequate provider for his family. Those thoughts sometimes led to self-doubt, which then made it even harder to make phone calls and send out letters. When those negative feelings started to build up, he'd schedule a meeting with Craig for some feedback and a motivational boost. He would also try to get more exercise and clear his head. As Craig told him, this could be a long and difficult process, but he wasn't going to feel any better about himself – or find a job – by sitting on the couch, watching soap operas and having a pity party.

He started attending the Lakeview Job-Hunters Club, the group that he learned about from the bookmark months ago.

They met on Wednesday mornings at a church not too far from his home. The group was led by a local Human Resources consultant who was a member of the church. The meetings were a lot like the 'group therapy' meetings at Genesis, but it was a different group of people. They shared success stories and suggestions. Bob had gotten a few referrals from the group and had made some friends. He was constantly surprised by the number and variety of people that were in the same boat he was. He also found himself helping new members with how to get their job searches started. While he hadn't found a job, he was now a veteran in the process.

There were minor successes. He had interviewed with several companies. In a few instances, he interviewed more than once and one time he was a finalist. But he didn't have any job offers and right now he didn't have any solid opportunities working.

Linda was getting nervous too. Last week they had removed a mole from her shoulder and they were still waiting on the biopsy results. The surgeon said that he didn't expect the mole to be cancerous, but they needed to wait for the test results. This worry, on top of everything else, was turning her into a wreck.

Bob's severance expired and they were now living off savings. He was able to continue his health insurance through COBRA, but it was costing over $1,500 per month. He needed to take his money out of National's 401(k) plan and was debating with himself about whether to roll the money into an IRA or to take the money and pay the tax penalty. He knew the right long-term answer was to roll it over, but he was afraid they would need the cash. He was also eligible for unemployment compensation, but somehow that felt like taking a handout and he didn't think he would be comfortable taking the money unless he really needed it. In the end, the need for cash outweighed his pride and he applied for unemployment, and he was glad he did.

After an anguished weekend, the results of the biopsy came back. As the surgeon had predicted, the mole was benign. Linda would be just fine. What a relief. After they got the results, Bob and Linda went to dinner at Antoine's, their favorite neighborhood restaurant, to celebrate. They talked about his job search and their future.

"Honey, we're coming up on a time when we'll need to make some hard choices." Bob had been avoiding this conversation. He didn't think either he or Linda would take it well. "As I see it, we've got two or three choices. I can keep trying to find a job, although after four months I'm getting pretty discouraged, or I can start looking out of town. Craig said the job market in Chicago is better – and so is Denver. If we're willing to relocate, there are more doors for me to knock on."

"You know I really don't want to move, and I know you don't either," Linda said quietly. "We've lived around here all of our lives. Our family and friends are here. The kids would hate leaving their friends and grandparents." She sighed. "You said you had three choices, but you only mentioned two. What else are you thinking about?"

"You remember when we were first married; I talked about opening a small bookkeeping shop. If I could get a few regular customers, I could make an okay living. It might not be what I was making at National, but it's a whole lot more than unemployment. I could work out of my office at home to keep expenses down." As Bob talked, his energy level went up and his confidence level improved.

Linda wasn't quite as confident. "I don't know, Bob. It seems like it would take a while to get started. What do we do in the meantime? I don't know if I can deal with our income changing every month. What would we do about insurance? I just need to think about it."

"I understand. The idea is only about half-baked anyway. I've had it in the back of my mind since I left National, but maybe we need to give it more thought. To me, it beats the heck out of moving."

Over the next week, Bob and Linda talked about the idea more and more. Bob spent some time organizing his home office and making notes. He talked with some friends, who had small businesses, about how they got started, and who was doing their bookkeeping. He got some leads for potential accounts. Maybe there was some promise to the idea after all.

For the next two weeks Bob worked hard on his business plan. He started by writing out some notes (figure 6). He selected a company name, 'Bookkeeping by Bob,' and asked a friend to design a logo. He ordered a second phone line and set up his home computer to serve as an answering/fax machine. He bought some stationery supplies and printed letterhead and business cards. He set up a business page on LinkedIn and looked into advertising on LinkedIn. Finally, he put together a small brochure that outlined the services he wanted to provide.

Next, Bob worked on simplified budgets for both his business and home. He needed to see what level of revenue he

Notes on Starting a Home-Based Business
1) Write business plan – know what I want to do
2) Conduct market research – know my competitors
3) Form an outside Board of Advisors. Listen to them
4) Be prepared to market and to sell
5) Research any applicable fees I might incur, including necessary registrations or licenses
6) No matter how busy I am, dedicate at least 20% of my time to new business development

(Figure 6)

would need to generate from the business to meet the financial demands of the household. He concluded that he would need between four and seven accounts, billing between five and ten hours per week per account. While he couldn't expect to start off that busy, he felt that if he could land two accounts in the first month, and add two per month over the next quarter, it would work. His last task was to start working on a list of people he would invite to serve on his Advisory Board. He knew that he might have difficulty staying objective at times and having a group of three or four business professionals that he could ask for advice would be very helpful.

With all that done, Bob hit the streets. He called on his potential referrals and told his story. On his third call, he landed a client! He was now the bookkeeper for a small antique shop. They had been doing the books themselves and the business had grown too complicated for them. It wouldn't bill the hours that Bob had hoped for, only two to three per week, but it was a start. Now he could call on others and call himself a legitimate business. After another week of sales calls, Bob picked up one other client. This one was a small manufacturer with eighteen employees. This one was right up Bob's alley and should produce a reasonable revenue stream. That night Bob and Linda celebrated.

"Linda, I'm really starting to get excited about this," Bob said with a big smile over dinner. They had gone back to Antoine's to celebrate. "I really think this is going to work."

Linda smiled back. "I'm very proud of you, Honey. But I thought you said you didn't like to sell. These last two weeks must have been very hard for you."

"I've got to admit that I'm not very comfortable with it, but it's okay. I've learned a lot from networking. I don't "sell." I just tell my story and try to find out how I can help them, and it's working. I've got two contracts and that was my goal for this month." Bob tried to sound reassuring, but his distaste for sales was obvious to Linda.

"How are we going to handle our health insurance?" Linda was trying to change the subject.

"We can stay on COBRA for now, and when the business is a little more stable, we can look for a personal policy. After I get a few employees, we can get a group policy for the company."

Linda's eyebrows went up. "Get a few employees? I thought you were still trying to get a few accounts. Won't it be awhile before you're ready to hire people?"

"Well, uh, sure. I need to build the business up a little first, but I thought maybe I could get an assistant and someone to do the sales part. That would free me up to do the stuff I'm really good at, the bookkeeping."

"Why don't you just take one step at a time?" Linda replied with a smile. "Until I see us making the house payment and buying groceries, I'm not excited about helping to feed other families."

"I understand," Bob said with mock frown. "I was just kind of dreaming. I am sure it will all work out pretty soon."

Bookkeeping by Bob did okay, but not great. Bob was able to get another small client, but then he stalled. Even though he kept calling on potential customers, he found they often had another service. It became clear he had not done enough market research before he started. He never guessed that there were so many firms just like his. The pressure to succeed was growing. He was trying to divide his time between marketing the business, researching potential accounts, servicing his existing accounts and still trying to keep his job search alive.

One afternoon, while working on a sticky accounting problem for his largest account, the phone rang.

Bob answered. "Bookkeeping by Bob. This is Bob, can I help you?"

"Bob, this is Gus Stanton from Warner Industries. How have you been?"

CHAPTER 11 – WHICH WAY TO GO?

Bob's heart skipped a beat. Gus Stanton had been his first networking contact months ago. They had stayed in touch for a while and Gus had given Bob several more names to follow up with. The last time they had talked, Gus had mentioned that there was something going on at Warner, but he had not been specific. Since it had been several months since they had talked, Bob had almost forgotten about it.

"Pretty good," answered Bob after catching his breath. "How about you?"

"Super, just super. Hey, how is your search coming?"

"It's taken an interesting turn lately. I wasn't having much success finding the right job, so I'm trying to get my own bookkeeping business going. It's been kind of a slow start, but it is starting to come together. I'm still working on the search, but not very seriously. I'm hopeful that this will work out." As he was saying this Bob wasn't sure if he was trying to convince Gus, or himself.

"That's great, Bob. I'm glad to hear that. I knew you'd land on your feet. I know you mentioned that there were some other accounting folks cut loose from National when you were. Do you know if any of them are still looking for a job?"

Bob's ears perked up. "I think there are one or two still in outplacement. I probably should be. Why do you ask?"

"Remember when we talked a couple of months ago and I mentioned that I thought we might have something cooking? Well, it's done. We've decided to bring on a new product line and need to expand our accounting department to handle it. I plan on hiring a new manager and then helping that person hire a new staff. The product is very similar to the types of things that National Products sells, so I thought you might know of someone that might be a good fit for this job."

Bob's mind was racing. What should he say? He just got his business started. Was he ready to dump it and go to work for Warner? What if he didn't get the job – would he be able to focus on the business again? Why had he started this at all? Maybe he should have stuck with his search. He took a deep breath and decided that just talking to Gus didn't mean he would be offered a job. Nor did it mean that he wouldn't be able to meet his clients' needs. "To tell you the truth, Gus. That sounds like a job that I might be interested in. Maybe we could talk some more about it."

"That's just what I was hoping you'd say," laughed Gus. "I don't want to take you away from your new business, but I think we've got a good opportunity here and I think you'd be a very good candidate. I'll tell you what; I'll send your resume down to our Human Resources department and ask them to bring you in for an interview. Then we'll see how things go from there. They will want to talk with you and maybe do some testing. If they agree you're a good match, then you and I will talk some more. You should expect a call in the next day or so."

"Great. That'll be just great, Gus. Thanks for calling and thanks for thinking of me." Bob hung up the phone and tried to deal with his conflicting emotions. He had been trying to get used to the idea of self-employment. He was looking forward to having more flexibility with his schedule – being his own boss – no morning commute – having an ownership in what he did. He also was worried. Could he find additional clients? He hated the sales part of the business. How long would it be before he would be able to replace the income he had with National? Warner Industries was a good firm and he thought that Gus Stanton would be a great guy to work for. He'd have stable hours, good pay and benefits. Which way should he go?

He thought back to Linda and her comment at dinner. "Why don't you just take one step at a time?" she had said. That was still sound advice. Until Gus extended an offer that Bob wanted to accept, there wasn't a decision to make. There was no use in worrying about the future, or "borrowing trouble" as his grandmother used to say. He simply needed to be ready to react when the time came. Bob turned back to his client's books and tried to not think about Warner Industries.

The next day a recruiter from Warner called and scheduled Bob for an interview and assessment testing the following day. On the way to his interview, Bob was as nervous as he had been for months. The recruiter knew that Gus Stanton was interested in Bob and so they had a friendly, and frank, conversation about employment with Warner and about Bob's background. Bob was relaxed and handled the questions well. His networking experience had been excellent preparation. He asked several good questions about Warner, several of which he already knew the answer to, but he wanted to get the recruiter's perspective. The interview lasted just under an hour and afterwards Bob felt it had gone well.

He also took two online assessments. One was a personality profile designed to see if his personality was a good fit with the demands of the job. The recruiter said that Warner had used this test for years and felt that it worked very well. The other test was an honesty test. This apparently was given to all applicants for positions in accounting, finance and cash management. Bob thought he did okay on both tests and hoped that the company would think so too.

After the testing, Bob met with the recruiter again. Bob was told that it would take a day or two to score the tests and he should hear from Warner early the following week. He drove home feeling good about his day, and even more conflicted about working for himself or for someone else.

The weekend was rainy, and Bob and Linda tried to make it a family-oriented weekend. They all went to a movie together and shopped for school clothes. They played miniature golf on an indoor course. Bob tried to put both Bookkeeping by Bob and Warner Industries out of his mind as much as possible. On Monday, Bob hung around his office waiting for the phone to ring but there was no call from Warner. The same thing happened Tuesday and he started to get discouraged.

When Bob returned home from the Lakeview Job-Hunters Club meeting Wednesday morning, he had a message on his answering machine to call Gus Stanton. He was so nervous he had to try three times before he dialed the number correctly.

"Gus, this is Bob Smith," Bob said after Gus answered. "I'm sorry I missed your call earlier, I was out of the office at a meeting. How was your weekend?"

"It was great, and so were your test results. Bob, we've talked a lot about you these last couple of days. We compared you to several other very good candidates and we think you're our man. I know we haven't talked salary or specifics yet, so I'd like to see if you can come down tomorrow afternoon and maybe we can work out some of the details and put together an offer you can't refuse. How's that sound to you?"

Bob's head was swimming. How could all of this happen so fast? He took a deep breath and tried not to sound too excited. "That sounds good, Gus. How about 2 o'clock?"

After he hung up, Bob called Stacy Rodney at Genesis. He told her the situation and scheduled some time to meet with her that afternoon and work on his negotiating skills. He then quickly returned some calls and drove down to meet Stacy.

"Bob, I am so excited for you!" Stacy was smiling almost as much as Bob was. "I know how hard you've worked on your search. It sounds like you may be close to the end of a long road – and the start of a new one. How do you feel?"

"To tell you the truth, I'm kind of confused. I really want this to go well with Warner Industries because it sounds like a perfect job for me. But, I'm really starting to like working for myself. I don't know which way to go." Bob relaxed a little when he said this. It felt good to say it out loud.

"Bob, that is perfectly understandable and normal. Keep in mind, there may be a way to do both. But first, we've got to get you ready for tomorrow so that you have the opportunity to make the decision. So let's talk about negotiations.

"I know you've negotiated things before. If you are like many people, when you think about negotiating you think about the last time you bought a car and it makes your skin crawl. Not all negotiations are that hard, especially when both sides want to reach a mutual agreement. Buying a car is often a one-time transaction. The salesman wants to maximize his commission and you want to minimize your expense. It can be difficult to get a win-win situation.

"Some people will tell you that negotiating a job offer is like that. I've heard people say that the first one who mentions a salary figure is the loser. I don't think that's true. While you may be talking about salary and benefits, what you're really negotiating is the beginning of a relationship that both of you hope lasts a long time. If either side tries to 'beat' the other side, or if either side thinks the other side is trying to 'beat' them, it won't work. You have to assume that the company is making an honest and fair offer that is within their salary structure. And you may have to make a reasonable counter-offer that meets your needs. If the company is trying to 'beat' you, you don't want to work there. That is not an environment that promotes company loyalty.

"But enough preaching – let's talk about some practical tips. To start with, you need to know what you want. On a piece of paper I want you to write out the terms and conditions that are ideal to you. Write down a job title, a set of job responsibilities, salary, benefits, vacation, etc. As you do that, be reasonable. No one is going to offer you a million dollars a year for this kind of job. At the same time, don't sell yourself short. You are framing your ideal offer and you can dream a little."

After Bob finished, Stacy continued, "Now, write down your absolute minimums. You may need to look hard at your family budget and talk this over with Linda. What is the lowest salary and benefit package you can live on? What if you don't get any vacation time for a year or two? How many hours per week are you willing to work? How much travel can you manage? You've got to know your bottom line so you know when to walk away. I don't expect this to happen with Warner Industries, but you have to be prepared.

"Now, your objective in these negotiations is to come as close as possible to your ideal offer, without being perceived as pushy or overly demanding. You'll have to recognize that Warner, or any company, probably has established pay ranges, benefit plans, and so on. Even if Gus Stanton wanted to give you what your ideal package is, he may not have the flexibility or authority. The way for you to succeed is to be flexible and creative.

"Remember, there is more to a job than a base salary. Be willing to make trade-offs. For instance, if the salary is a little below what you'd like, maybe you can pick up an extra week of vacation as an offset, or maybe you can ask for a hiring bonus. That will get you the earnings you want in the first year and let you prove your performance so that you can get a good raise for the second year. Possibly there is, or could be, an incentive plan or an improvement to the benefits plan. Most employers won't mind if you ask these questions. They also won't suggest them if they don't need to.

"Very importantly, be respectful of whatever is offered. Make sure you understand the entire package, including the job responsibilities and potential career path. If you don't like the package they offer, don't say no. Ask for time to consider it – maybe talk it over with your wife. That will give you time to really analyze things and make a good, fair counter-offer. Even if the offer is a dream, don't leave anything on the table. Take the time to think about it. Both you and Warner have invested a lot of time in the search process. One or two more days are not going to be a problem.

"Most importantly, like everything else in your job search, be yourself. Don't accept a job offer that doesn't feel good to you. Don't try to be something you're not. If you strive to do what is right for you, then when you get a job offer that fits you, you'll have a winner."

With Stacy's help, Bob refined his ideal offer and his minimum requirements. He also promised Stacy that he would talk about both lists with Linda that night. Then they worked through a couple of practice interviews and negotiating sessions.

Bob did talk with Linda that night and with a few modifications they agreed on both his ideal offer and his walk-away points. He then reviewed his notes from that afternoon (Figure 7) and by the next afternoon he was ready for his meeting with Gus Stanton.

"Bob, it's good to see you again." Gus welcomed Bob into his office and offered him a chair. "I'm glad you wanted to talk more about this. This is such a super opportunity and I am convinced that you're the right guy for us. Do you have any questions about anything?"

I'm Fired?!?

What Bob really wanted to ask was 'how much money?' but instead he asked a few questions about reporting relationships, work hours, travel, professional dues, continuing education and benefits. These were all issues on his wish list. The answers he got were acceptable on most accounts, and outstanding on others. Finally the money issue broke the surface.

"Bob, why don't we talk salary for a minute?" Gus smiled as he said this. Bob's paranoia-meter was in full swing and he wasn't sure he liked that smile. "Tell me, what did they pay you at National Products?' This was a question that Bob and Stacy had worked on yesterday. "Gus, if you're like me, you hate to

	Negotiating Notes
	1) Write down my ideal job offer (be reasonable)
	2) Write down my minimum requirements
	3) Seriously consider all offers
	4) Be creative
	5) Don't be afraid to ask for more if the offer is not sufficient
	6) Don't be greedy

(Figure 7)

talk about things like salary. What I was paid at National was based on a lot of things like performance, seniority, and their interpretation of the market rate for my job. Instead of talking about my salary, let me tell you my salary range. Since I had been there for several years and my performance met or exceeded expectations, understand that I was paid in the upper half of this range." Bob then told Gus the minimum and maximum of his pay range at National Products.

"Okay, I can appreciate that, Bob," Gus said making some notes. "Did you have any incentive or bonus opportunities?"

"I was eligible for a company-wide profit sharing plan. Over the last five years or so that plan had paid between two and fifteen percent of salary. The average was around five percent." Bob was a little more relaxed now that he could see that this approach had not offended Gus.

"How about benefits?" Gus asked.

Bob described the major benefit plans as well as the amounts he'd had to pay for his share of medical insurance, etc. He also described National's 401(k) plan.

"Overall that sounds like a pretty good package you had," said Gus. "From what I can see, I think we're pretty close. Let me show you what we're thinking." He handed Bob an offer letter with the salary and benefits detailed. "As you can see we have a salary range that is slightly lower than what you had, and I will assume the salary is a little lower also. However, we do have an incentive plan tied to this position. The normal payout for this plan, assuming you meet your objectives, is ten percent of salary and can go higher if you exceed expectations. We charge a little less for insurance than National but it looks like their 401(k) plan may be slightly richer than ours. All in all, I think we're in the same ballpark. What do you think?"

"I think this looks very fair," answered Bob with a smile. "I appreciate your offer very much and the confidence you've shown in me. I think this would be an excellent place to work and to build my career. Do you mind if I sleep on this – maybe talk it over with my wife?"

"Not at all. In fact I would have been disappointed if you hadn't. I'm always suspicious about people who make snap decisions about important matters like this. Please, take your time and call me in a day or two and let me know what you think."

Bob and Gus wrapped up their meeting with a short discussion about the upcoming weekend weather and Bob headed for home. The offer wasn't the dream offer he had hoped for, but it wasn't as bad as he had worried about.

That evening Bob and Linda went out to dinner. Over dessert they talked about the offer. Linda didn't seem as interested as Bob was. "I just don't think it's enough money, Bob. That salary is 15% less than you were making at National. I know that there is a bonus, but there isn't any guarantee, and even then you won't get the money until the end of the year. We would really feel that pinch in our monthly budget."

"I understand that, Honey, but there are some trade-offs. We'd spend about $100 less per month on insurance, and it's closer to home, so I'd spend less on gas and car repairs. The Educational Assistance Plan is good too. I've been talking about getting my Master's Degree. Now I can – and have Warner pay for it."

"What about your business? You were just starting to get that going. Do you really want to go back to working for someone else?"

"I've thought a lot about that these last few days. I enjoy the flexibility of working out of the house, but I don't like the sales side. If someone would bring me all the business I need, and guarantee me enough to earn a good living, I think I'd love it. But right now it's frustrating. I spent some time this afternoon looking hard at my accounts. Two of them are so small that even if I do everything for them I still don't make any money. I'm better off helping them to find someone else to do the work for them.

"The third account is taking ten to fifteen hours per week and is fairly profitable. I'm sure that I can take this job and do the books for this client on evenings or weekends. That will keep the business open and I can still take some deductions off our taxes. Plus the extra money won't hurt and the hours are flexible. I can work them around the kids' schedule without any problem."

Linda thought about that idea for a few moments. "That's good, but I'm still worried about the money. Couldn't you ask for a little bit more? If they'd come up five or ten percent, then with your business you'd be about the same place as with National. Then with the bonus, maybe we'd even be a little better off. Maybe you can ask for some more vacation too. We've already talked about skiing next spring. If we have to wait a year for a vacation, we'll lose both the spring and next summer. The kids are counting on going somewhere."

Bob sighed. "I know what you mean. I was looking forward to the Rockies too. Okay, I'll talk with Gus tomorrow and tell him that I like the offer. I just want to ask for two changes, a ten percent increase in the base pay, and two weeks of vacation starting in the first year. How's that sound?"

"That would be wonderful, Bob." Linda smiled. "I am so looking forward to having this all behind us."

"Me too, Honey, me too."

The next day Bob called Gus Stanton and made his requests. Gus couldn't do everything Bob asked for, but after a short discussion they settled on a five-percent increase in the base pay plus a five percent signing bonus payable after 90 days of acceptable performance. Gus also agreed to one week of paid vacation and one week of unpaid vacation in the first year.

After touching base with Linda, Bob agreed, and two weeks later he started his new job as Accounting Manager for Warner Industries.

CHAPTER 12 – LESSONS LEARNED

"So, Bob, how was your first week? Everything you'd hoped for?" Gus Stanton was standing in Bob's office door. Bob's desk was covered with papers and he was looking a little harried.

"Everything and more!" Bob grinned. "It has been a busy and hectic week, but I think I'm going to love it. The people have been wonderful and the work is very interesting. I've never created my own team before. We've talked to some really good applicants this week. I'm really looking forward to what's coming down the road – even if I don't know what it is."

"That's super, Bob. I'm really glad to have you on the team. Have a super weekend and don't work too late." Gus waved as he walked away.

"Same to you!" Bob shouted behind him. Then he leaned back and smiled at his clutter. It felt good to be up to his neck in work again. He really did think he was going to love this job. This week he had also been able to transfer his two small accounts to another bookkeeping firm for the same fee structure that Bob had negotiated. The prior week he had spoken with his primary account and they were fine with using his now part-time bookkeeping business.

This weekend Bob planned to finish his thank-you letters. He was sending a brief letter to each of the people he had networked with to thank them for their help and tell them about his new position. He would also make sure to let them know to call him when they needed help. He also needed to update his LinkedIn profile. Now that he had all those contacts he wanted them to know he'd landed with Warner.

Don and Barbara Howell came over to dinner on Saturday night. While Bob and Don sat on the deck that evening, Bob talked about his job search and some of the things he'd learned. "You know, Don, I sincerely hope I keep this job until I retire, but now I know I will survive if I don't. I now know that I prefer being employed to being unemployed. I've also learned to always keep my resume up to date. Despite my best intentions, you just never know what might happen.

"I will also work to keep my network alive. I met some really great people over the last five months and they helped me a lot. Maybe someday I can help them, or maybe someday I'll need to ask them for help again. In either case, it pays to stay in touch.

"I need to work harder on my financial planning. This job change caught me by surprise. I wish I'd had more money in savings. We never ran out, but it gave Linda plenty to worry about. I need to have a better program to set money aside for a rainy day or two, and for retirement.

"I'm going to use Warner's Educational Assistance Plan and go back to school. There were several jobs I looked at where an MBA would have been a big help. Everyone needs to continue learning and keep current. It is also a big help in the job market.

I'm Fired?!?

"Finally, I need to spend time with my family and good friends, like you. The support I've had has been wonderful. I never really thought about all of the people that care about me and want me to succeed. It has been an emotional time and I couldn't have done it alone. Thank you. Thanks for everything."

"You're welcome, Bob," said Don. "I know this was a tough period for you, but I also knew you'd get through it. Congratulations, and well done!"

The End

My Reflections

As you might have guessed, this is a quasi-autobiographical story. I have been on the "wrong side" of mergers, acquisitions and reductions in force six times. Those six times have given me the opportunity to examine my career and become more comfortable with a process that many have not experienced. Reflecting back on my history, and Bob's story, here are ten important ideas that I hope you keep in mind as you begin your job search.

Manage Yourself Before You Try To Manage Your Search

When you got the news that you just lost your job, it probably felt like someone just punched you in the stomach. Even when you think you know it's coming, the finality is often hard to bear. The first thing to do is to remember to breathe. Stay calm and let the reality sink in. Take the time to talk with your employer to truly understand what happened and why. If you are in control of your emotions, you are more likely to understand the details about how your final pay and benefits will be processed, what support the company might provide, when you can clean out your desk, etc.

Don't scream, don't shout and don't try to find someone to blame. While you may not feel that you should have been fired, your former employer can be a great help in helping you find a new job. Be civil and don't burn your bridges. You'll need them to provide references and, who knows, maybe you'll want to work for this company again in the future. If you need to vent your frustration, save it for later with a sympathetic friend.

Get control of your emotions, let the anger go, and start working on your future. When you interview – and you will – don't bad-mouth your former employer. That only suggests that if things don't work out, you will be talking badly about them in the future.

Identify Your Transferrable Skills

Whether you are fresh out of college, or have been in your job for many years, you may not have the exact experience a recruiter is looking for. Every recruiter would like to find a candidate who has done this job before because it means less training time and more productivity. But just because you might not have done that specific job does not mean that you do not have the necessary skills. For instance, a busy stay-at-home mom may have developed great skills at scheduling, prioritizing and managing a budget. A skilled machine operator might know how to measure and track quality. A former lifeguard might be comfortable working in a hectic environment where good judgment and quick decision making is important. These are all skills that can be transferred to different jobs and future employers need to know that you have those skills.

The bottom line is – don't sell yourself short by limiting your job search to what you've already done. Carefully evaluate your skills and seek out jobs that use those skills, even if you are using them in different ways.

Spend Some Time Reflecting

An important part of your job search is getting to know yourself. You will be asked many different questions while interviewing. You can answer them best if you are prepared, and a key part of your preparation is figuring out what you want. Spend some quiet time reflecting on who you are, what you do well, what you need to do better, and what you want to do. Know yourself, including both your strengths and your limitations. If you are comfortable in your own skin, that comfort will be reflected as confidence in your interviews.

Think about keeping a journal during your search. This is a great way to keep track of what worked and what didn't. It also can be helpful, if not therapeutic, to put your thoughts, feelings and frustrations on paper. The act of writing things down provides a clarity you won't get just by thinking about things.

Many local unemployment offices will offer free career assessments. These tests can help you identify jobs or careers that align with your skills and interests. These tests also may open your eyes to a career path that you had not considered. Talk with people who have very different jobs than you have, to really understand what they do and what skills are required.

Most importantly, spending some quality time with "the man in the mirror" will help to ensure that you are prepared. As

Ben Stein says, "The indispensable first step to getting the things you want out of life is this: decide what you want."

Be True To Yourself

You have been out of work for a while and you just want a job. There are bills to pay and food to buy. There is a point where you'll do just about anything simply to get back to work. My message here is to be true to yourself. If you take a job that you know you'll hate, you will hate it, and it will show. Ultimately, the job will end badly and you'll be unemployed again.

While you may need to take a job that is less than the job you want, don't just take any job. Keep looking for a job that has value and that you can be proud of. It may be basic labor, or it may be well below your skill set or education, but make sure it is a job that is compatible with your values. Don't take a job that you wouldn't want to tell your mother about.

Honesty Is Always the Best Policy

Often I hear stories about people who have "enhanced" or "inflated" their resumes. Sometimes they claim more education than they really have, or maybe they claim to have worked somewhere longer or had more responsibilities than actual. I even know of one case where an applicant claimed to have played professional baseball, when he really hadn't. I won't advocate that you list every fact about your career on your resume, but I will advocate that everything on your resume should be true.

Basing a job on a lie is a bad way to start off and can have disastrous consequences. Employers have the legal right to terminate someone who falsifies their application. What would you rather be telling a future employer, I was laid off or I was fired for lying?

Don't Be Afraid To Ask For Help

The important reality that underlies networking is that if you ask for help, people will give it to you. If you don't ask for it, don't expect to receive it. When my father entered the workforce, most people expected to stay with one company until they retired. When I began my career almost 30 years ago, I could have reasonably expected to work for two or three companies and have a fairly straight career path. Some of my contemporaries are still working for the same companies they joined straight out of college – but not many. Today's graduates can expect not only to change jobs every few years, but to change careers several times. It's just the way things are.

This means that the chances are very high that many of the people you will interview with will have been in your shoes sometime in their career. Quite possibly, they have been laid off or RIFed, and have used networking to find their next job. There no longer is a negative stigma associated with being caught up in a reduction in force. Don't be ashamed that you are unemployed and don't be afraid to ask for help – most people will be happy to do what they can.

Manage Your Finances and Your Pride

There are realities that come with being unemployed. Many of these revolve around pride and money. Because of pride, some people don't want to apply for Unemployment Compensation. Because of pride, and maybe an inflated sense of self-worth, some people might not take a job that is a step backwards in their career. Because of pride, some people won't consider a reduction in pay or a reduced work schedule.

Pride, when expressed as self-confidence, can be a very powerful emotion and it can be very helpful in finding the right job. But when pride overwhelms common sense, it could cause you to lose your house or be unable to feed your family. Most of us need to work to provide the income necessary to pay the rent, buy food and clothing, and to send our children to college. So, if your job search stretches longer than your savings, you may need to swallow your pride and take a job that is not your dream job. As I mentioned earlier, don't take a job you know you'll hate, but be willing to take a job that can meet at least part of your financial needs. A future employer will be impressed to see that you've had the determination to keep working while you continue to look for the right job.

In difficult times like these, you may need to take a step back in your career and a corresponding reduction in your earnings. If you can find that job – take it. Use that opportunity to re-evaluate your career. Possibly your past experience will position you to move up quickly with your new employer. If not, keep your network alive and continue to look for what you want, but in the meantime you can put food on the table.

Keep Yourself Busy

Getting laid off is not a forced vacation. Looking for a job is a full-time job, and may be one of the hardest jobs you will ever have. If you find yourself out of work, don't let yourself fall into a habit of sleeping in and watching TV all day. Get up like you are going to work, get dressed and go to work finding a job. Keep up your routines and keep up your energy level. If you find that you have free time, try volunteer work – this can be very rewarding and lead to some great networking contacts. Spend some extra time exercising and improving your health – the old axiom is true, when you look good, you feel good – and if you feel good, you'll interview better.

Lying around the house feeling sorry for yourself will not get you another job. Getting up and getting busy is the only way to get back to work.

Diversify Your Search

I frequently hear people talk about looking in the newspaper want ads every day, or surfing the Internet looking for jobs. In this book I advocate networking as a key component of your job search. Some people look for "help wanted" signs in windows. My suggestion here is that you cannot simply do one or two of these things – you need to do all of them. While networking may give you access to the huge array of unadvertised jobs, you can't walk away from the ones that are advertised. You should regularly look at the want ads in your local papers – especially any local job-oriented papers. Also check every Internet job board you can find. Many of these are linked and share jobs, but some are not. Look for industry-specific job boards. Read trade magazines and look at their websites for links to relevant jobs. Visit your local Unemployment Office to learn how to access their job postings. Go to company websites and see if they have jobs posted there. Walk in to companies that you are interested in and ask if they are hiring.

The important lesson is to not limit your search to the one or two techniques where you feel most comfortable. Instead, stretch yourself and look in every possible corner, under every available rock. Somewhere out there is a job for you, and it won't come to you by itself, you've got to go find it.

Remember the Golden Rule

It may happen quickly, or it may take longer than you had hoped, but you will find another job. When that happens, you need to do three things. The first is to thank everyone who helped you. Let them know where you landed and what you're doing. Express your appreciation for the support, advice and encouragement that you received along the way.

The second thing you need to do is to reverse your role. You can now be the one giving advice and encouragement. You can be the one who shares contacts and helps other people learn to network. You are now the experienced veteran that can mentor the rookie. Give back as much as you received.

And finally, maintain your network. Stay in touch with those people you met. You could send them a quarterly email just to touch base or occasionally meet for lunch just to check in. Keep your LinkedIn profile current and post updates occasionally. The important concept is to stay in touch. In these harsh economic times, you never know when you might need that network again, and you don't want to have to start all over. It is much easier to maintain a network than to create a new one.

This book is one way I've tried to follow my own advice. I am deeply indebted to those who have given me advice and counsel – those who have been willing to spend time with me and listen to my story – and especially to those whose help led me to find my next job. I hope this book helps you in many of the same ways.

– – Roger Dusing – –

APPENDIX A – 30 Interview Questions You Need to be Ready to Answer

Every interviewer has his or her favorite questions, so you can never be fully prepared, but in this section you'll find 30 questions that could apply to just about any job. I encourage you to write out answers to these questions and practice saying those answers out loud. This process will give you confidence and improve the quality of your answers. I expect you'll also find that while someone may not ask the questions as I've written them here, you can find at least part of an answer in one of these questions.

1. In your job, have you ever had a customer that was out of control? Think of the most difficult customer service situation of that type that's ever happened and tell me how you handled it.

2. What types of experiences have you had in talking with customers or clients; specifically, tell me about a time when you had to communicate under difficult circumstances?

3. Describe a situation where you felt it was necessary to break company policy or alter standard procedure.

4. Think of a specific day when you had lots of things to do and tell me how you organized your day.

5. Tell me about a time when you were part of team that had a particularly difficult goal to achieve. What was your role in helping the team be successful?

6. Tell me about a specific thing you did in your last job that was creative.

7. Tell me about a time when you had to make a quick decision that you were proud of.

8. Tell me about the best manager you ever worked for – what was it that made him/her a great person for you? Now the other side of the coin – who was your "worst" boss and why?

9. Tell me about a goal you set for yourself in the past and how successful you were in accomplishing that.

10. You've heard the expression "being able to roll with the punches." Tell me about a time that you've had to do that when dealing with a difficult person or situation.

11. When you had a job to do that was particularly uninteresting, how did you deal with that?

12. What experience have you had with a miscommunication with a customer or a fellow employee?

13. I'm sure there was a time that you and a coworker simply didn't get along. Tell me about that situation – what was the source of the conflict and what did you do to make the situation better?

14. In your past job experience, tell me about a time when you stuck to company policy or procedure in order to solve a problem when it might have been easier not to.

15. You've indicated that you can be decisive in most situations and that's excellent. But now I want you to tell me about a time when you felt you've had a problem making a decision. How did you deal with that?

16. Tell me about a time when you had to admit that there was a situation that you couldn't handle.

17. Describe a tough decision that you've made when no policy existed to cover it, and tell me what you did.

18. Tell me about at time when you weren't successful in a tough decision you had to make.

19. Describe a time when you had to communicate some unpleasant feelings to a manager and how you did it.

20. Tell me about a time when you had a direct report who was being unsuccessful and what you did to help them improve their performance and turn it around? Conversely, tell me about a time when you were unsuccessful and you had to terminate the employee.

21. Tell me about a time when you didn't communicate something unpleasant but should have.

22. Tell me about a time when the corporate culture fit you like a glove. What was it that made that such a great place for you to work? Now what about the flip-side – a time when you were very uncomfortable with the culture?

23. What was one obstacle you had to overcome in your last job and how did you do it? How about an obstacle in your last job that you were not able to overcome?

24. Give me an example of a time when working with financial details was difficult for you. How did you handle it?

25. Tell me about a time when you were faced with a stressful situation at work. How did you handle it?

26. Give me an example of a project that you worked on that you were really proud of. Tell me specifically what you did.

27. Nobody is perfect, so describe a mistake you made on your last job and how you corrected it.

28. Give me an example of when you had to provide leadership.

29. Think of a time when you didn't handle a customer's problem well. Tell me what happened.

30. Now that you've had a chance to review the essential functions of the job, is there any reason that you wouldn't be able to perform the duties listed?

APPENDIX B – Sample Resume Accomplishments

One section on the resume that many people find challenging is the accomplishments section. Included here are some examples from a wide variety of industries and positions. Your goal is not to use these on your resume, but to use these examples to help you craft accomplishments based on your work experience. Remember to quantify everything you can.

- Improved customer inquiry response time by developing and implementing process improvements to facilitate phone- and email-based query management.

- Achieved a $2,500 monthly savings for XYZ Company within three months of hire by streamlining procedures.

- As manager of the product marketing team, successfully oversaw the entire marketing program implementation for a $50 million product line.

- Consistently grew revenue and profits in a rapidly changing environment through aggressive cold-calling, persistent follow-up, and relationship-focused account management.

- Contributed to growing customer base by forging strong relationships with potential new clients.

- Created a Succession Planning process for a 500-employee company that identified successors and high-potential employees and directed developmental needs to prepare participants for their next assignment.

- Created internal structures to support corporate charitable giving resulting in increased donations of money, materials and volunteer time.

- Designed and implemented an improved file management system that reduced file retrieval backlog from four days to one.

- Developed a tracking and call-back system for delinquent accounts that reduced A/R collection period by 50 percent.

- Developed and handled marketing campaigns and budgets for a variety of businesses in different industries and markets.

- Developed communications strategy to respond to customers regarding a new 235-item product list, resulting in a 15 percent decrease in the number of returned orders.

- Dramatically increased pass rate of eighth-grade students from 67 percent to a record high of 93 percent on state proficiency testing.

- Established office procedures supporting a 200 percent increase in medical staff with no subsequent increase in support personnel.

- Extensive merger and acquisition experience from both sides of the table, including due diligence and integration activities.

- Facilitated corporate strategic and operational planning, yielding specific and measurable corporate, departmental and personal goals, and ensuring that all managers had direct line-of-sight expectations.

- Improved office efficiency and customer service by overhauling previously haphazard filing system.

- Increased sales by 50 percent over the previous year.

- Initiated a neighborhood watch program covering a seven-block area. Recruited over 75 volunteers, scheduled shifts, and publicized the effort to the local paper. Crime dropped over 18 percent in the first six months.

- Initiated and implemented a strategy for consolidating computer operations from three centers to two, saving $200,000 without interrupting processing.

- Integrally involved in seamless migration of 1,000-plus users from various local servers onto corporate UNIX servers in aggressive one-month timeframe.

- Managed a sales territory covering eight states, successfully meeting sales goals and increasing overall sales by 15 percent per year through cold calling and direct customer referrals.

- Managed a staff of 14 employees who successfully improved productivity by 15 percent while also reducing operating costs by over $1 million.

- Prepared and mailed invoices (average 150 per week) and processed incoming payments (average $125,000 per week) consistently error free and 100 percent on time.

- Prepared complete, precise, accurate designs of precision electronic equipment using the latest CAD/CAM software, which resulted in a 25 percent reduction in overall design flaws.

- Produced total meal sales 20 percent higher than those of the other servers in the restaurant.

- Presented 10 storytelling workshops for grade levels K-6 at county schools and public libraries. Trained over 100 after-school group leaders on how to start a storytelling program, resulting in self-sustaining programs at five locations.

- Received numerous customer comments and correspondence – as well as a company bonus – in recognition for exemplary customer service.

- Reduced insurance expenses by $15,000 in a single year by re-negotiating malpractice, health and disability insurance policies.

- Served a customer base of 150, the largest on firm's customer-service team.

- Served as Medical Editor on 14 annual trade-show daily newspapers, reporting on daily activities and trade show events, consistently meeting client expectations and all related deadlines.

- Ten years' experience managing 15 employees across multiple territories on the East coast. Effectively managed P&L of $10 million business unit. Consistently generated 30-35 percent gross profit.

- Wrote three successful grant applications to private foundations, resulting in funding to serve an additional 100 clients.

Roger Dusing

APPENDIX C – Bob's First Resume

Robert M. Smith
1285 Pleasant View Drive
Plainville, IN 46238
Cell: 317-996-0214 Home: 317-270-0108

Objective
To obtain long term employment with a well-established organization where I may fully utilize my accounting and management skills and abilities.

Experience

National Products, Inc. — Plainville, IN
Accounting Manager — 09/2006-03/2011
- Managed staff of 5 accountants and clerks.
- Directed all accounts payable activities.
- Assisted with the annual inventory of supplies and equipment.

Lead Accountant — 05/2001-09/2006
- Processed G/L transactions.
- Managed check reconciliations.

Accountant — 02/1996-05/2001
- Processed G/L transactions.
- Supported billing by researching discrepancies.

Acme Manufacturing — Plainville, IN
Accountant — 08/1991-01/1996
- Processed check reconciliations.
- Assisted with special projects for maintenance division.

Education

University of Phoenix - Online — Indianapolis, IN
MBA candidate — In Progress

Bingham College — Summerset, IN
Bachelor of Science in Accounting — 1991

Skills
- Computer and Internet literate; 10-key by touch
- Assertive, self-motivated, goal-oriented, organized and efficient.
- Flexible, cooperative, hard working, team player and reliable.
- A good morale builder.

References
Professional and personal references available upon request

I'm Fired?!?

APPENDIX D – Bob's Revised Resume

Robert M. Smith
1285 Pleasant View Drive • Plainville, IN 55555
Home: 718-555-5555 • Cell: 917-555-5556
bob.smith@gmail.com

Summary

- Experienced Accounting Manager with specialized skills in overseeing a complex manufacturing general ledger
- Skilled manager with proven skills in improving departmental performance and reducing employee turnover

Accomplishments

- Implemented consistent check reconciliation process of over 1,000 checks per month resulting in reduced bank fees, 99.5 percent accuracy and increased collections of $150,000 per month
- Directed all accounts payable activities involving three A/P Specialists processing in excess of $1 million in monthly disbursements to over 700 vendors with 99 percent accuracy
- Implemented internal audit procedures resulting in improved control over internal expenses and saving $250,000 per quarter
- Automated G/L transaction processing reducing financial statement preparation time by three business days and ensuring 100% on-time production of statements
- Assisted in the selection and implementation of new G/L system, improving financial work flows and saving $375,000 in departmental expenses

Work Experience

National Products, Inc. — Plainville, IN	Accounting Manager	2006 to 2011
	Lead Accountant	2001 to 2006
	Accountant	1996 to 2001
Acme Manufacturing — Plainville, IN	Accountant	1991 to 1996

Education

University of Phoenix – Online – Indianapolis, IN	MBA	In Progress
Bingham College — Somerset, IN	BS Accounting	1991

References
Professional and personal references available upon request

ABOUT THE AUTHOR

Roger Dusing is a 30-year Human Resources executive who has been on both sides of mergers, acquisitions and reductions-in-force. Working in a wide variety of industries, including higher education, manufacturing, financial services, retail and publishing, he has become an experienced manager, leader, executive coach, and consultant. He has first-hand experience finding jobs and helping others find theirs.

Roger earned a Bachelor of Science in Industrial Engineering from Bradley University, a Master of Science in Administration from Central Michigan University, and is currently pursuing a Ph.D. in Business from Northcentral University. He has held the Senior Professional in Human Resources certification since 1991.

He is a currently a practicing Human Resources Executive and lives in Liberty, Missouri.

PRAISE FOR *I'M FIRED?!?*

"Having unfortunately experienced both sides of the downsizing process several times myself, I have a true appreciation for the dynamics at play as either employee or employer during a downsizing or restructuring. I think *I'm Fired?!?* should be handed out to every employee by their company at the time of reduction-in-force notification. Roger has taken a unique and very human approach to covering all aspects of the emotional and challenging process of being terminated, moving through the stages of recovery and productive search. Most books on finding a job focus simply on a step-by-step set of actions to take and do not deal with the human element which is so fundamental, completely normal, yet critical in completing a successful job search."
Cam Bishop,
Publishing/Advertising Industry Executive

"*I'm Fired?!?* provides practical tips from an HR professional who understands the roadblocks to employment, and the human side of losing a job and paycheck. This book is a good textbook for the newly-unemployed, and for the HR professionals whose job includes looking across the desk and telling co-workers that their paycheck and job have ended. I recommend *I'm Fired?!?* for professionals and for workers struggling to cope with an unwelcome change."
Joseph Colantuono, Labor Attorney

"HR Managers and Business Owners, when you must tell someone the sad news about his/her position being eliminated; you **MUST** give him/her this book. It is an honest story about the emotions and challenges someone grapples with when thrust into the new job search process. Roger's writing is candid, compelling, crisp, practical and insightful. He has the perfect mix of storytelling and useful 'what-to-do' lists. This book is at the top of my 'must read' list of management and personal development books."

***Ted Davis*,**
Leadership Consultant and Educator

"*I'm Fired?!?* is a valuable primer about the stages of career transition. This practical, easy-to-read fable is a realistic portrayal of the journey on which those who are between jobs must embark, and the emotional rollercoaster they most certainly will experience."

***Richard E. Beyer*, Human Resources Executive, Former Kansas State Secretary of Labor**

"*I'm Fired?!?* is very much on point, very personal, very instructive, and very valuable. A must read for anyone in job transition. Transition is always an opportunity to find better application of your skills and experience…to go for alignment and excitement in work. Read this and be encouraged!"

***J. Allen*,**
International Management Consultant

I'm Fired?!?

"*I'm Fired?!?* reflects the outplacement experience well. I worked with Roger 20+ years ago as an outplacement coach and have followed his career since. This is an excellent read for anyone anticipating outplacement or is facing uncertainty in the outplacement process. Much of the challenge is mental, psychological and emotional. Roger explores it all well in this book."
***Michael Shirley*,**
Career & Search Executive

"*I'm Fired?!?* is an informational resource as well as an emotional trip for those of us who read the text and lived the moment during our career journey.

It is poignant, instructive and at times a difficult and uncomfortable memory of the unemployment journey many of us have faced this past decade. Roger captured the fear, the uncertainty and the recovery of the journey.

This is an important read for those who have lost their careers and are transitioning, those who may need to prepare for job loss in this uncertain economy, and for those who simply want to understand what individuals faced with the need to change are going through."
***Leslie G. Griffen*, MCDP, M.A.,**
Outplacement Industry Executive

From the Foreword…

"Having spent much of my own career as a job search and career transition consultant with two major outplacement firms, I can attest that readers of *I'm Fired?!?* will be well advised. I welcome this heartfelt and enlightening contribution to our collective library of job search literature."

Leigh Branham,
Author/Consultant/Career Counselor
Author of:

Re-Engage – How America's Best Places To Work Inspire Extra Effort In Extraordinary Times, with Mark Hischfeld (2010) McGraw Hill

The 7 Hidden Reasons Employees Leave – How To Recognize The Subtle Signs and Act Before It's Too Late (2005) AMACOM

Keeping The People That Keep You In Business – 24 Ways to Hang On to Your Most Valuable Talent (2001) AMACOM